Emma Poole • Caroline Reynolds • Bob Woodcock

ESSENTIALS

Year 9
KS3 Science

oursebook

How to Use this Coursebook

A Note to the Teacher

This is the third of three science coursebooks for students in Key Stage 3.

Together, the coursebooks for Years 7, 8 and 9 provide full coverage of the programme of study for Key Stage 3 science.

Each coursebook comprises...
- clear, concise content appropriate to that year
- questions and tasks to reinforce students' learning and help improve their confidence.

This Year 9 coursebook is split into 12 topics. The topics are colour-coded to show which of the following headings they come under:
- Disease, Changing the Environment and Behaviour (green)
- Reactions of Metals, Environmental Chemistry and Using Chemistry (red)
- Electricity, Speed and Forces (blue).

Each topic consists of seven pages.

The first four pages of a topic contain the content students need to learn. They feature...
- **key words** picked out in colour in the text and listed in a box at the end of each topic
- a **Quick Test** to test understanding.

The final three pages in a topic contain questions and exercises to reinforce students' understanding and provide skills practice:
- **Key Words Exercise** – requires students to match the key words to their definitions.
- **Comprehension** – requires students to answer questions based on a passage that explores the nature, history and understanding of the scientific ideas introduced in the topic.
- **Testing Understanding** – comprises a literacy exercise, and another exercise to develop skills such as the interpretation of graphs and data.
- **Skills Practice** – devoted to a relevant investigation to develop the students' investigative skills. The students can just answer the questions, or carry out the investigation before answering the questions.

A pull-out answer book, which contains the answers to all the questions in this coursebook, is included.

Each coursebook is supported by a workbook to provide further practice and help consolidate students' learning.

A Note to the Student

We're sure you'll enjoy using this coursebook, but follow these helpful hints to make the most of it:
- Try to learn what all the key words mean.
- The tick boxes on the contents page let you track your progress: simply put a tick in the box next to each topic when you're confident that you know it.

- Try to write your answers in good English, using correct punctuation and good sentence construction. Read what you have written to make sure it makes sense.
- Think carefully when drawing graphs. Always make sure you have accurately labelled your axes and that you have plotted points accurately.

Contents

Disruption of Life Processes

Disease

The seven processes of life, which can be remembered by the term 'Mrs Gren', are...

- **m**ovement
- **r**espiration
- **s**ensitivity
- **g**rowth
- **r**eproduction
- **e**xcretion
- **n**utrition.

A variety of factors can stop these seven processes working efficiently. If any of the processes are disrupted, then you can suffer from illness or disease.

Biological Factors

Microorganisms (microbes) like bacteria, fungi and viruses can affect the way your body works. Disease-causing microbes are called pathogens.

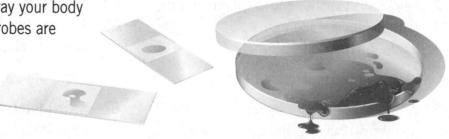

Pathogen Type	Examples and Effects
Bacterial	• Some forms of meningitis – meningitis affects the membranes in the brain and this can cause brain cells to die, therefore disrupting many of the life processes. • Weil's disease – caught from contact with rat urine and can affect the excretory system by damaging the liver and kidneys. • Syphilis – causes ulcers on the reproductive organs that can spread to other areas of the body.
Viral	• Influenza ('flu') – causes sore throats and headaches, affecting respiration. • HIV (Human Immunodeficiency Virus) – attacks the immune system and can allow any infection to damage any part of the bodily processes. • Mumps – causes the swelling of salivary glands, which affects the digestive system.
Fungal	• Ringworm – affects the growth of the skin, appearing like a raised reddish ring on the skin. • Athlete's foot – affects movement by causing itchy, flaking skin, especially on feet and toes (although it can affect other areas).

Smoking and the Lungs

Tobacco smoke contains chemicals that affect several bodily processes. The lungs are particularly affected.

Oxygen from the air and carbon dioxide from the blood are exchanged in the lungs. The oxygen is used for respiration and the carbon dioxide is the waste gas produced.

The lungs are adapted for gaseous exchange by having a very large surface area and thin walls that are near to many blood capillaries. This allows the gases to diffuse in and out of the blood.

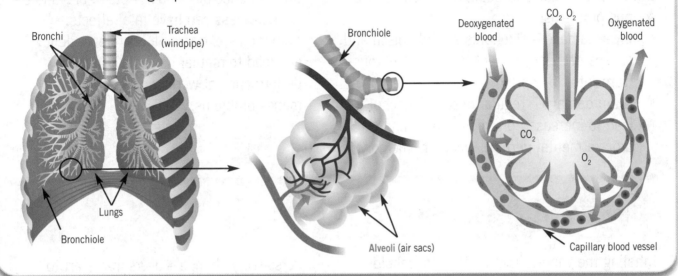

Bronchi

Trachea (windpipe)

Lungs

Bronchiole

Bronchiole

Alveoli (air sacs)

Deoxygenated blood

CO_2 O_2

Oxygenated blood

CO_2

O_2

Capillary blood vessel

The Effects of Smoking

Tobacco smoke disrupts the way in which organs, especially the lungs, work.

You can see the brown tarry deposit left if the smoke is passed through cotton wool in the apparatus shown opposite.

To vacuum pump

Cotton wool

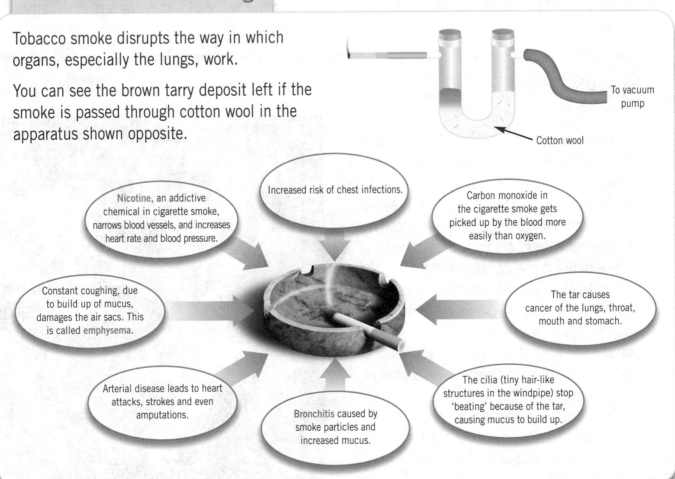

Nicotine, an addictive chemical in cigarette smoke, narrows blood vessels, and increases heart rate and blood pressure.

Increased risk of chest infections.

Carbon monoxide in the cigarette smoke gets picked up by the blood more easily than oxygen.

Constant coughing, due to build up of mucus, damages the air sacs. This is called emphysema.

The tar causes cancer of the lungs, throat, mouth and stomach.

Arterial disease leads to heart attacks, strokes and even amputations.

Bronchitis caused by smoke particles and increased mucus.

The cilia (tiny hair-like structures in the windpipe) stop 'beating' because of the tar, causing mucus to build up.

Disruption of Life Processes

The Effects of Alcohol

In moderation, alcohol is relatively harmless. But alcohol abuse and dependency can cause serious problems:

- Liver damage – alcohol is a mild poison and causes parts of the liver to become fibrous (turn into fibres) and therefore useless.
- Brain damage – regular doses of alcohol lead to increased brain-cell death and a drop in mental performance, e.g. memory.
- Impaired judgement – this occurs while under the influence of alcohol. Acts of bravado or foolhardiness can have fatal effects.
- Addiction – extreme alcohol dependency can lead to regular days off, reduced performance at work, violence and money problems.

The Effects of Solvents

Inhaling the vapour from certain household substances, such as glues and paints, can cause problems:

- Hallucinations – users may lose their grip on reality.
- Personality change – users may start to display different personality traits.
- Damage to organs (e.g. the lungs, brain, liver and kidneys) – this damage is usually permanent.

The Effects of Other Drugs

Other drugs can also affect bodily processes:

- Hallucinogens (e.g. Ecstasy, L.S.D.) – these cause hallucinations and, in the case of Ecstasy, the feeling of being full of energy, which can lead to dehydration and collapse.
- Depressants (e.g. alcohol, barbiturates) – these depress the nervous system.
- Stimulants (e.g. amphetamine, methedrine, cocaine and crack) – users become psychologically and physically dependent on the feelings of energy that stimulants can cause. They can also cause a change in personality.
- Pain killers (e.g. heroin, morphine) – these can cause addiction and complete collapse of personality and self-discipline.

Natural Barriers to Disruption

Your body has natural defences that help to stop processes being disrupted:

- Your skin is slightly acidic (pH 5.5), which will kill many microbes. The skin is also a physical barrier.
- You produce sweat, tears and ear wax, which can all destroy microbes.
- If you get a cut, blood clots seal the wound.
- Your windpipe (trachea) is lined with mucus, which traps microbes, and has tiny hairs (cilia) that move the microbes up and into the oesophagus.
- Your stomach contains acid that kills microbes.

If any microbes get past these defences, your white blood cells can...

- dissolve, or engulf and digest, the microbes
- produce antitoxins that work against poisons made by invading microbes
- produce antibodies that stick to the microbes to stop them working.

Once invaded, the body 'remembers' the disease and can make the antibodies again very quickly if needed. This is called immunity.

Antibodies can be passed on to unborn babies through the placenta and to young babies through the breast milk, making them immune too.

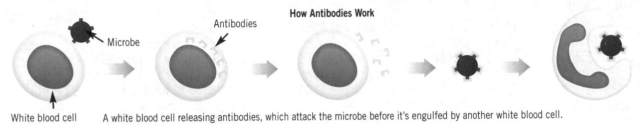

How Antibodies Work

Microbe · Antibodies · White blood cell

A white blood cell releasing antibodies, which attack the microbe before it's engulfed by another white blood cell.

Artificial Barriers to Disruption

You can be immunised against a disease:

- You can have an injection of weakened or dead microbes that cause your body to make antibodies. This will protect you in future. An example is the anti-HPV vaccine (against cervical cancer), which is only made up of virus-like particles.

- You can also be injected with the antibodies themselves. These are often produced in laboratory-bred animals. This type of vaccine usually requires regular booster doses and doesn't last for life. An example is the anti-tetanus vaccine.

Quick Test

1. What is a pathogen?
2. What three types of microbe can cause disease?
3. What is the addictive drug in tobacco?
4. What are the air sacs at the end of the bronchioles called?
5. Alcohol affects which two organs the most?
6. What are passed onto babies in breast milk to give them immunity from a microbe?

KEY WORDS
Make sure you understand these words before moving on!

- Alveoli
- Antibodies
- Antitoxins
- Bronchitis
- Emphysema
- Hallucinogens
- Immunity
- Nicotine
- Pathogen
- Vaccine

Disruption of Life Processes

Key Words Exercise

Match each key word to its meaning.

Key Word	Meaning
Alveoli	Protection from disease by the production of antibodies
Antibodies	A collection of dead or weakened microbes, or antibodies, injected to give protection
Antitoxins	The air sacs where oxygen enters and carbon dioxide leaves the blood
Bronchitis	Substances produced by white blood cells that can neutralise a specific microbe
Emphysema	An addictive chemical found in cigarette smoke
Hallucinogens	Chemicals that neutralise a poison produced by a microbe
Immunity	A smoking-related disease caused by excessive mucus and smoke particles
Nicotine	A condition in which air sacs are damaged due to constant coughing
Pathogen	A disease-causing microbe
Vaccine	Substances that cause hallucinations

Comprehension

Read the passage about a study into the causes of lung cancer, then answer the following questions.

1. How might advertising be used to create the impression that smoking is 'cool'?

2. Describe several ways in which the 'smoking group' and the 'control group' should have been identical in order to make this a fair test.

3. Why do you think that the results of the study provoked a hostile reaction from the tobacco companies?

4. Comment on the following statement: "Being a smoker means that you will definitely get lung cancer at some stage."

Scientists investigating the increase in deaths from lung cancer during the 1940s and 1950s began to suspect that the underlying cause was related to smoking. At the time, many people assumed that smoking was safe and thought that it was rather sophisticated – an impression that was reinforced through heavy advertising by the tobacco companies.

A major study compared a group of smokers and a group of non-smokers over a long period of time. The study showed that the smokers were more likely to get lung cancer than the non-smokers, and that the more a person smoked, the greater their chances were of getting lung cancer.

The non-smokers in this study were called the 'control group' and were chosen so as to differ from the smoking group in the fact that they had never smoked. The results of the study provoked a hostile reaction from the tobacco companies and came as a shock to many people. However, it took many years to build up public awareness of the dangers of smoking, partly due to the cigarette manufacturers' huge advertising budgets.

Testing Understanding

1 **Fill in the missing words to complete the sentences about the disruption of life processes.**

a) There are three types of microbe that can cause disease: _____,
_____ and _____.

b) Meningitis is caused by _____. Mumps is caused by _____
and athlete's foot is caused by _____.

c) Once microbes are inside the body, you depend on your _____
_____ cells to 'fight' them. Some produce _____ that
neutralise poisons; others produce _____ that _____ to
microbes to prevent them working. Others may dissolve them, or engulf and
_____ them.

d) Immunity can be given either by catching the disease or by _____, where
weakened or _____ microbes are injected, or by the injection
of _____ made outside the body.

e) The body can also be damaged by the abuse of drugs like _____,
which is legal but can damage the liver and brain. There has also been an increase in the
use of illegal _____, such as Ecstasy and cocaine. Users can become
dependent on, or get _____ to, these drugs.

2 **Study the table about smoking and lung cancer, then answer the questions that follow.**

Year	Lung Cancer Deaths per 100 000 Men	Cigarettes Smoked per Man per Year
1900	10	800
1920	25	2050
1940	50	4000
1960	175	3500
1980	160	3000

a) Plot the above data onto two separate
graph grids as line graphs, with the year
on the x-axis.

b) What conclusion can be drawn from the
results about the number of cigarettes
smoked per man per year?

c) What conclusion can be drawn from
the results about the number of lung
cancer deaths?

Disruption of Life Processes

Karen and Daniel set up an investigation into the effects of an antibiotic drug, penicillin, on the growth of bacteria.

First they inoculated a Petri dish containing agar jelly with bacteria and allowed it to grow over the plate. They then placed four discs of blotting paper onto the surface.

Each disc was soaked in a known concentration of the antibiotic. They thought that the antibiotic would kill the bacteria on the plate.

After one week, they looked at the dish and could see areas where the bacteria had disappeared. The pattern they could see was as shown below.

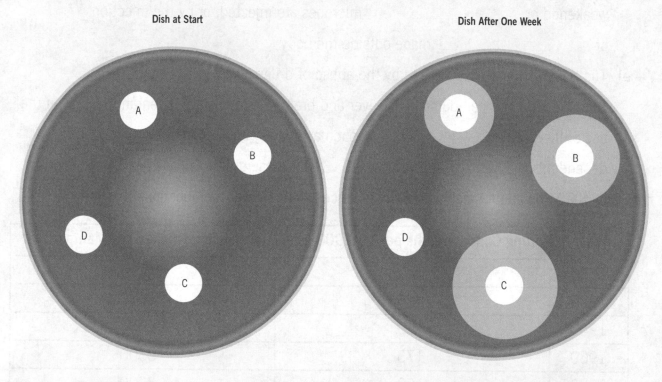

Dish at Start   **Dish After One Week**

1. Karen and Daniel could see that the area around each disc was different, but how could they measure this?

2. Which disc had the greatest concentration of penicillin on it?

3. Disc D showed no difference. This was because they had only soaked it in water. Why would they do this?

4. They had to carry out this investigation very carefully. Why would they need to be especially careful when doing this?

5. After carrying out each stage of the investigation, both pupils had to wash their hands in antiseptic soap. Why was this necessary?

Metals and Metal Compounds

Properties of Metals

Metals have special properties because of the way their atoms are arranged. These special properties make metals very useful, for example:

- Copper is a good thermal and electrical conductor, and is very resistant to corrosion. It's used to make water pipes and saucepans, and is used in electrical wiring.
- Aluminium has a low density and is very resistant to corrosion. It's used to make drinks cans and bicycle frames.

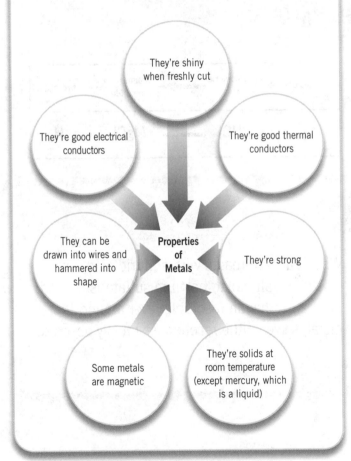

Properties of Non-Metals

These are some of the characteristic properties of non-metals:

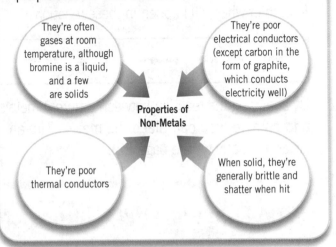

Symbols and Formulae

Every **element** can be represented by a simple one or two-letter code. For example, copper has the **symbol** Cu and aluminium has the symbol Al. A chemical **formula** shows the type and number of atoms in the smallest particle of a substance.

Three commonly used **acids** are hydrochloric acid (HCl), sulfuric acid (H_2SO_4) and nitric acid (HNO_3). The chemical formulae of these acids show that they contain the element **hydrogen** (H), which is true of all acids.

Chemical symbols allow scientists who speak different languages to communicate with each other. This allows them to share developments and understanding.

Evidence of a Chemical Reaction

In a chemical reaction, new substances are made. Evidence that a chemical reaction has taken place includes...

- a change in colour
- a change in temperature
- bubbles that show a gas is being made.

Metals and Metal Compounds

How Metals React with Acids

Some metals react with acids, forming a salt and releasing hydrogen gas. This equation allows you to predict what will happen in these reactions:

metal **+** acid ⟶ salt **+** hydrogen

By analysing the reaction between different metals and an acid, you can place the metals into an order of reactivity (see page 32).

Copper is a very unreactive metal and doesn't react with acids, so no bubbles of hydrogen are seen.

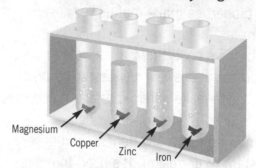

Magnesium   Copper   Zinc   Iron

The Reaction with Hydrochloric Acid

Metals react with hydrochloric acid to form chloride salts. Magnesium reacts with hydrochloric acid to form magnesium chloride and hydrogen gas. Lots of bubbles of hydrogen can be seen. Heat is also given out and the test tube becomes warmer.

magnesium **+** hydrochloric acid ⟶ magnesium chloride **+** hydrogen

$$Mg + 2HCl \longrightarrow MgCl_2 + H_2$$

The Reaction with Sulfuric Acid

Metals react with sulfuric acid to form sulfate salts. Here is an example with zinc:

zinc **+** sulfuric acid ⟶ zinc sulfate **+** hydrogen

$$Zn + H_2SO_4 \longrightarrow ZnSO_4 + H_2$$

When calcium reacts with sulfuric acid, an **insoluble** salt called calcium sulfate is formed. The salt forms an insoluble layer around the metal, so very little reaction is actually observed.

The Reaction with Nitric Acid

Metals react with nitric acid to form nitrate salts. Here is an example with zinc:

zinc **+** nitric acid ⟶ zinc nitrate **+** hydrogen

$$Zn + 2HNO_3 \longrightarrow Zn(NO_3)_2 + H_2$$

Note the brackets followed by the number 2 in the formula for zinc nitrate. This means that everything inside the brackets is multiplied by two, so the smallest particle of zinc nitrate contains one zinc atom, two nitrogen atoms and six oxygen atoms.

How Metal Carbonates React with Acids

Metal carbonates...
- contain atoms of a metal, carbon and oxygen
- react with acids to form a salt, water and **carbon dioxide** gas
- form chloride salts when reacting with hydrochloric acid, sulfate salts when reacting with sulfuric acid, and nitrate salts when reacting with nitric acid.

$$metal\ carbonate + acid \longrightarrow salt + water + carbon\ dioxide$$

This is the reaction between calcium carbonate ($CaCO_3$) and hydrochloric acid:

$$calcium\ carbonate + hydrochloric\ acid \longrightarrow calcium\ chloride + water + carbon\ dioxide$$

$$CaCO_3 + 2HCl \longrightarrow CaCl_2 + H_2O + CO_2$$

Reacting metal carbonates with acids can be used to make salts of less reactive metals like copper, which don't react directly with acids.

Identifying Hydrogen and Carbon Dioxide

You can tell hydrogen or carbon dioxide gas has been produced in a reaction because...
- hydrogen is a flammable gas that burns with a squeaky pop
- carbon dioxide turns limewater cloudy.

Gas	Test	Result if Gas is Present
H_2	Place a lighted splint near by	Burns with a squeaky pop
CO_2	Bubble through limewater	Limewater turns cloudy

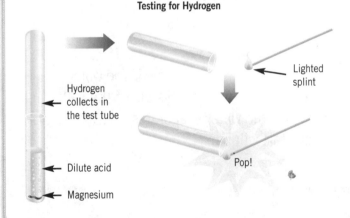

Testing for Hydrogen

Hydrogen collects in the test tube

Lighted splint

Dilute acid

Magnesium

Pop!

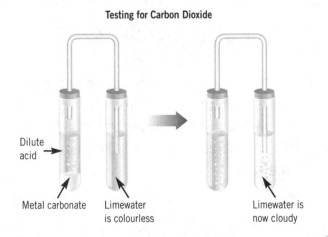

Testing for Carbon Dioxide

Dilute acid

Metal carbonate

Limewater is colourless

Limewater is now cloudy

How Metal Oxides React with Acids

Metal oxides...
- contain atoms of a metal and of oxygen
- react with acids to form a salt and water
- form chloride salts when reacting with hydrochloric acid, sulfate salts with sulfuric acid, and nitrate salts with nitric acid.

$$metal\ oxide + acid \longrightarrow salt + water$$

For example, copper oxide reacts with sulfuric acid to form the salt copper sulfate and water:

$$copper\ oxide + sulfuric\ acid \longrightarrow copper\ sulfate + water$$

$$CuO + H_2SO_4 \longrightarrow CuSO_4 + H_2O$$

Metals and Metal Compounds

Adding Acids to Alkalis

Acids and bases are chemical opposites. Metal carbonates, metal oxides and metal hydroxides are bases. Some metal oxides and hydroxides are soluble in water. Soluble bases are known as **alkalis**.

Two commonly used alkalis are...
* sodium hydroxide (NaOH)
* potassium hydroxide (KOH).

If exactly the right amount of acid is added to an alkali, a neutralisation reaction takes place and salt and water are made.

For example, hydrochloric acid reacts with the alkali sodium hydroxide to form the salt sodium chloride and water:

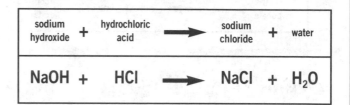

Again, the type of salt formed depends on whether hydrochloric acid, sulfuric acid or nitric acid is used.

Separating Soluble Salts

The salts formed in a reaction can be separated:
* First the solution is filtered to remove any unreacted metal or metal compound (because it's insoluble). This leaves the soluble salt and water.
* The solution is then warmed. The water **evaporates** to leave crystals of the salt. The slower the water evaporates, the larger the crystals will be.

Quick Test

1. Name the gas produced when a metal reacts with an acid.
2. Name the salt produced when zinc metal reacts with sulfuric acid.
3. Name the salt produced when sodium carbonate reacts with hydrochloric acid.
4. Name the salt produced when copper oxide reacts with nitric acid.
5. What is the general equation for the reaction between an alkali and an acid.

KEY WORDS
Make sure you understand these words before moving on!
* Acid
* Alkali
* Carbon dioxide
* Element
* Evaporates
* Formula
* Hydrogen
* Insoluble
* Metal carbonate
* Symbol

Key Words Exercise

Match each key word with its meaning.

Acid	A soluble base
Alkali	A chemical compound that contains metal, carbon and oxygen atoms
Carbon dioxide	Doesn't dissolve
Element	Turns from a liquid to a gas
Evaporates	The chemical opposite of bases; these compounds all contain the element hydrogen
Formula	A one or two-letter code used to represent an element
Hydrogen	A substance that's made of only one type of atom
Insoluble	A gas, produced when a metal carbonate reacts with an acid, which turns limewater cloudy
Metal carbonate	A way of representing the type and number of atoms in the smallest particle of a substance
Symbol	A gas, produced when a metal reacts with an acid, which burns with a squeaky pop

Comprehension

Read the passage about salt, then answer the following questions.

1 What is the chemical name for salt?

2 Name three foodstuffs that may contain surprisingly high levels of salt.

3 What is the recommended daily salt allowance for an adult?

4 How much salt should children under the age of 11 have in their diet?

5 How many deaths are caused by strokes in England each year?

6 Name four health problems that are linked to high blood pressure.

Sodium chloride is better known as table salt or simply 'salt'. Most of the salt you consume is already in the foods when you buy them. This means that the total amount of salt in your diet can be much higher than you think.

It's easy to guess that foods that taste salty, such as crisps, may contain quite high levels of salt. But other foods, such as some breakfast cereals, ready-made sandwiches and pasta sauces, contain surprisingly high levels of salt too.

The recommended daily allowance of salt for children over the age of 11 and adults is only 6g, and it's better to have less than this amount. Younger children should have less salt and babies should have less than 1g of salt a day. If children are allowed to consume larger amounts of salt, it can damage their health.

Eating too much salt can cause serious health problems. It can cause high blood pressure, which increases the risk of suffering a stroke. A stroke is a serious medical condition, which causes 50 000 deaths in England every year. Someone with high blood pressure is three times more likely to suffer a stroke. High blood pressure also increases your chance of suffering heart disease. High blood pressure can also cause damage to your eyes and kidneys.

Metals and Metal Compounds

Testing Understanding

1 **Fill in the missing words to complete the sentences about metals and metal compounds.**

a) Metals are _____ conductors of heat and electricity. Only one non-metal

element, carbon in the form of _____, conducts electricity.

b) The chemical formula of a substance tells us the _____ and number of

atoms present in the smallest particle of a substance. Sulfuric acid has the formula H_2SO_4.

This means that the smallest particle of sulfuric acid contains _____ hydrogen

atoms, _____ sulfur atom and _____ oxygen atoms.

c) Some metals react with acids to form a salt and a gas called _____. This

gas can be identified because it burns with a _____ pop. Magnesium reacts

with nitric acid to form a salt called magnesium _____ and hydrogen gas.

d) Metal carbonates react with acids to form a _____, water and carbon

dioxide gas. Carbon dioxide can be identified because it turns _____ cloudy.

e) Metal oxides and hydroxides also react with acids. They form a salt and _____.

Copper oxide reacts with hydrochloric acid to form a salt called copper _____

and water. No bubbles are seen during this reaction because no _____ is made.

2 **Answer the following questions about iron, which is a very useful metal.**

a) Complete the word equation below to show the reaction between iron and hydrochloric acid.

iron + hydrochloric acid ⟶ _____ + _____

b) When iron carbonate reacts with hydrochloric acid, a gas called carbon dioxide is produced.
How could you prove that this gas is really carbon dioxide?

c) Iron can be made into stainless steel. Stainless steel is an alloy (a mixture of metals). A
sample of stainless steel contains 70% iron, 10% nickel and 20% chromium. Copy and
complete the pie chart below to show the composition of this sample of stainless steel.
Remember to add labels.

George wants to investigate the factors affecting rusting. The table below describes what the substances in the test tubes do.

Substance	What it Does
Calcium chloride	Removes water
Boiled water	The water doesn't contain oxygen
Layer of oil	Stops oxygen entering the water

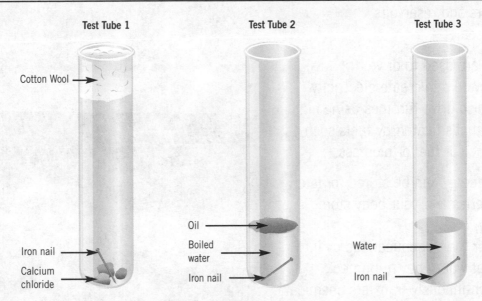

1 Copy and complete the table below by writing **yes** or **no** in each box to show the conditions experienced by the nails inside each test tube.

Test Tube	Any Water?	Any Oxygen?
1		
2		
3		

George leaves the nails in the test tubes for two weeks and then examines them. His results are in the table below.

Test Tube	Appearance of the Nail
1	No rust
2	No rust
3	Nail is very rusty

2 Write a conclusion for George's experiment.

3 George repeats his experiment but this time he uses iron nails that have been coated in oil. Describe how you would expect the nail in test tube 3 to look. Explain your answer.

Energy and Electricity

Where Electrical Energy Comes From

Energy can be harnessed from...
- the wind
- the Sun
- water in rivers and reservoirs
- tides in the sea.

Wind and water are used to drive **turbines**, which turn **generators** to create electricity. Power stations also drive turbines using high pressure steam that's heated by fuels such as coal, gas, oil, nuclear fuel or biomass.

Some forms of energy can be stored for later use. Fuels, batteries and your body store chemical energy:
- Fuels transfer their chemical energy into light and heat when they're burned.
- Your body continuously transfers chemical energy into other forms in order to grow, to move and to keep warm.

Wind Turbines

Solar Panels

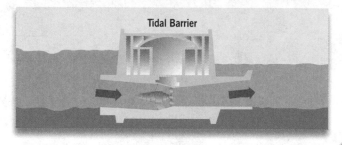

Tidal Barrier

Measuring Electrical Energy

Batteries and cells transfer chemical energy into electrical energy when they're connected in a circuit:
- A device called a voltmeter can measure the energy being transferred from the cell to the electric current.
- A bulb in a circuit transfers electrical energy into heat and light.
- A second voltmeter can be used to measure the energy being transferred from the current to the bulb.

Voltmeters measure a quantity called **potential difference**. The unit of potential difference is volts (V).

The voltmeters in the circuit below both show a reading of 2.5V. The amount of energy transferred from the cell to the current is equal to the amount of energy transferred from the current to the bulb. This shows that energy is conserved.

Electrical Energy from Power Stations and Generators

Electricity is usually generated in a power station by rotating a coil of wire between the poles of a magnet:

- The rotation of the coil of wire between the poles of the magnet produces a current in the coil of wire. The magnet and coil of wire together are known as a generator because they generate or create electric current.

- The rotating coil is driven by a turbine that's blown around by high pressure steam. The steam is produced by water that's heated by burning fuel or by a nuclear reaction.

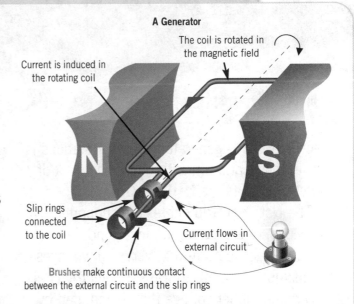

A Generator

Current is induced in the rotating coil

The coil is rotated in the magnetic field

N   S

Slip rings connected to the coil

Current flows in external circuit

Brushes make continuous contact between the external circuit and the slip rings

How a Thermal Power Station Works

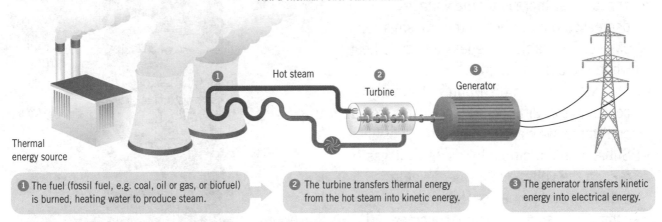

Hot steam

Turbine

Generator

Thermal energy source

❶ The fuel (fossil fuel, e.g. coal, oil or gas, or biofuel) is burned, heating water to produce steam.

❷ The turbine transfers thermal energy from the hot steam into kinetic energy.

❸ The generator transfers kinetic energy into electrical energy.

Electrical Current

There are two types of electrical current:

- Generators produce a current that changes direction every time the magnet turns. This is called AC, or **alternating current**. AC is the current supplied to homes.

- Current supplied by a cell or battery is known as DC, or **direct current**.

AC and DC current can be displayed on a screen.

AC Current

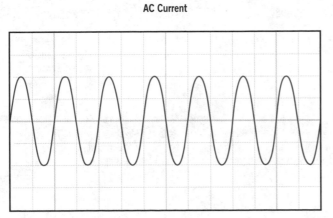

DC Current

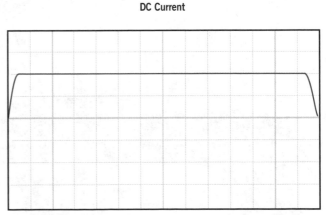

Energy and Electricity

How Electrical Energy Reaches Your Home

Electricity that's generated in power stations is sent to towns and cities through a network of cables known as the **National Grid**:

- The National Grid cables are supported by pylons, or are buried underground. They carry electric current at very high voltages.
- It's more efficient to transmit electricity at a much higher voltage than is required by consumers. Increasing the voltage decreases the current in the transmission cables. The cables lose less energy to heat when the current is lower.
- The National Grid distributes electricity to consumers at different voltages using step-up and step-down **transformers** in the **substations**.
- Substations in cities, towns and villages reduce the voltage to a safer level for industrial and home use. Different consumers, such as factories, homes and schools, require different voltages. The **mains electricity** that comes to your home is at a voltage of 230–240V.
- Electricity meters measure the electrical energy used in each house. Wires inside the walls carry the current to the electric sockets and lights.

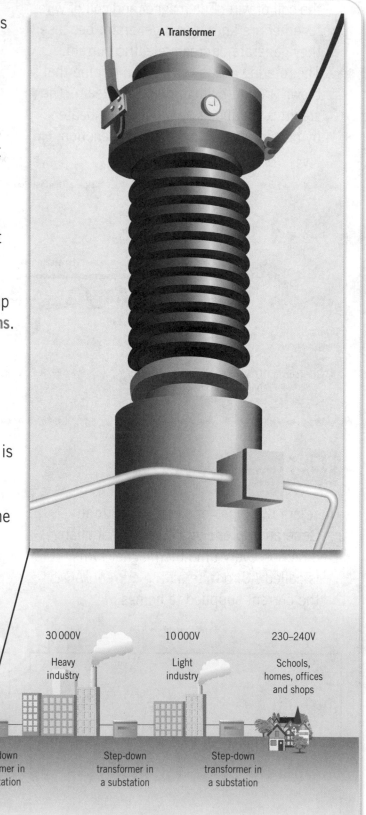

A Transformer

Distributing Electricity

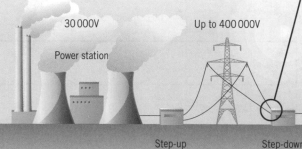

30 000V	Up to 400 000V	30 000V	10 000V	230–240V
Power station		Heavy industry	Light industry	Schools, homes, offices and shops
	Step-up transformer in a substation	Step-down transformer in a substation	Step-down transformer in a substation	Step-down transformer in a substation

Mains Electricity

Anything that transfers energy from one form to another is called a **device**:

- Devices that use electrical energy include toasters, hair dryers, fans, computers, kettles and DVD players.
- Whenever you plug in a device, you're connecting it into an electrical circuit.

In the UK, three-pin plugs are used to connect a device to a mains circuit. Plugs contain a fuse and each pin is connected to a wire:

- The live wire controls the AC current, flowing backwards and forwards many times per second.
- The neutral wire completes the circuit.
- The earth wire is a safety wire that connects the metal casing of a device to the earth. The earth wire works with the fuse to protect anyone who uses the device. If a loose wire inside the device touches the metal casing, a large current immediately flows through the earth wire and the fuse blows. This disconnects the circuit, preventing a possible electric shock or overheating that could cause a fire.

Most modern devices are made of plastic. This adds another layer of insulation because plastic is an electrical insulator. This is called **double insulation**. Devices with double insulation don't need an earth wire connected to the casing.

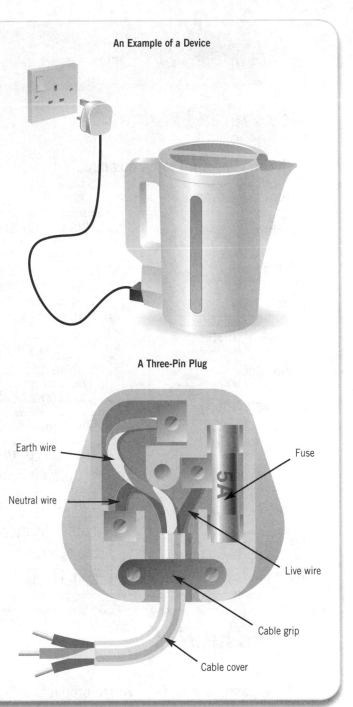

An Example of a Device

A Three-Pin Plug

Earth wire

Neutral wire

Fuse

Live wire

Cable grip

Cable cover

Quick Test

1. Name three different sources of energy.
2. Name three ways that energy can be stored for later use.
3. What is the unit of potential difference?
4. What is DC current?
5. What is AC current?

Energy and Electricity

Key Words Exercise

Match each key word to its meaning.

Key word	Meaning
Alternating current	A coil of wire rotating between the poles of a magnet
Brushes	This usually drives a generator in a power station
Device	This electricity comes to your home at 230–240V
Direct current	A device with a plastic casing
Double insulated	This changes the voltage to a safer level for use in homes
Generator	This tells you how much energy is transferred in a cell or in a bulb in an electric circuit
Mains electricity	A network of cables taking electricity from power stations to homes
National Grid	Something that transfers energy from one form to another
Potential difference	The parts of the National Grid that contain step-up or step-down transformers
Substations	Current that continuously changes direction, created by a generator
Transformer	These ensure continuous contact of the wires in a generator as the coil rotates
Turbine	Current supplied by a cell or battery

Comprehension

Read the passage about the waste products of electricity generation, then answer the questions.

1. Describe an effect of a polluting gas on the environment.

2. Give three disadvantages of wind turbines.

3. a) Give one advantage of using nuclear fuel to produce electricity.

   b) Give one disadvantage of using nuclear fuel to produce electricity.

Burning fossil fuels, such as oil, coal and gas, always produces waste. Waste gases can pollute the air, soil and water. Some polluting gases, such as carbon dioxide, increase the greenhouse effect and lead to global warming.

Renewable sources produce less pollution but can create other problems for the environment. Wind turbines change the landscape and produce loud noises that can disturb wildlife. Wind turbines only generate a small amount of electricity – one power station running on solid fuel generates about 2000 times more energy than a wind turbine. Also, another source of energy is required when the wind isn't blowing.

Nuclear fuel is a very efficient way of producing electrical energy and releases no harmful gases into the atmosphere. However, nuclear waste material needs to be disposed of safely, which can be very expensive. Many people also worry about the risk of accidental emission of radioactive material.

Testing Understanding

1 **Fill in the missing words to complete the sentences about energy and electricity.**

a) Electricity is generated in _____ and sent to towns

and cities through a network of _____ known as the

_____ _____. The cables are supported by

_____, or are buried underground. They carry electric current at very

_____ voltages.

b) It's more efficient to transmit _____ at much higher voltages than is

required by _____ and factories. Increasing the voltage decreases the

_____ in the transmission cables. The cables lose _____

energy to _____ when the current is lower.

c) Step-up and _____ transformers are used at _____ to

reduce the voltage to a _____ level for industrial and home use. The

_____ electricity that we use in our homes is at a voltage of 230–240V.

2 **The diagram below shows a correctly wired three-pin plug.**

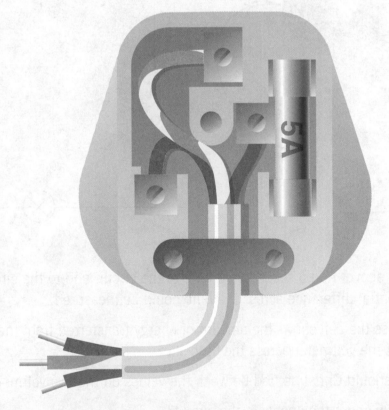

a) Label the live wire, the neutral wire, the earth wire and the fuse in the diagram.
b) Describe and explain the functions of the live wire and the neutral wire.
c) Many domestic devices are double insulated. What does this mean?
d) Which wire in a three-pin plug isn't required if a device is double insulated?

Energy and Electricity

Christine wants to investigate how the energy supplied by cells is used in an electric circuit. She set up the circuit below to measure the potential difference across a cell with a voltmeter in a simple circuit.

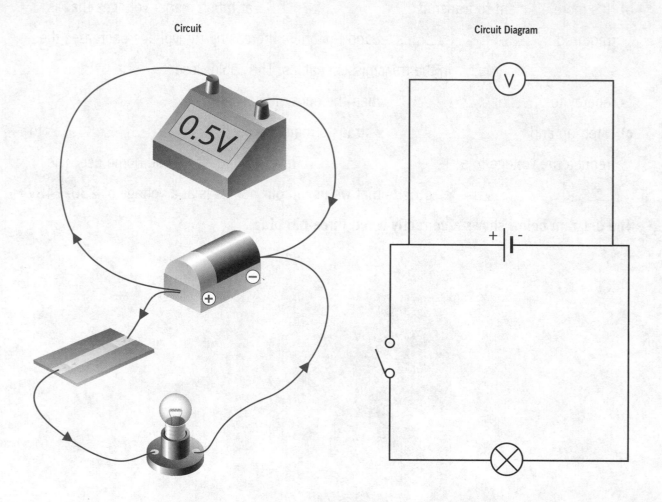

Circuit

Circuit Diagram

1. Copy the diagrams above. Add a second voltmeter to the circuit and to the circuit diagram to show how the potential difference across the bulb could be measured.

2. The voltmeter across the cell shows the amount of energy transferred from the cell to the current. What does the voltmeter across the bulb show?

3. What relationship should Christine find between the values on the two voltmeters?

4. What does this show about the energy in the circuit?

5. Christine adds a second cell next to the first cell in series. Draw a circuit diagram that shows how she can investigate whether energy is conserved in this circuit.

6. How would you expect the values of the potential difference to change?

Variety in the Environment

Sexual Reproduction and Variation

In order to reproduce sexually, organisms must produce specialised cells called **gametes**:

- Gametes are the 'sex cells' – eggs and sperm in animals, and ovules and pollen in plants.
- The nuclei of these cells contain DNA, which carries the genetic information determining the characteristics that will be inherited.
- When the nuclei fuse at fertilisation, the cell that's produced carries genes from both parents, resulting in a new individual.

Sexual reproduction means that...

- the genetic information from both gametes is passed on to the new individual
- the characteristics of the offspring are similar to the parents, but show quite a lot of differences to them.

Some of the differences between an individual and its parents may be an advantage (e.g. being taller may help in basketball) or a disadvantage (e.g. being taller may make it uncomfortable to drive a small car). Other differences may be neither an advantage nor a disadvantage.

Fertilisation

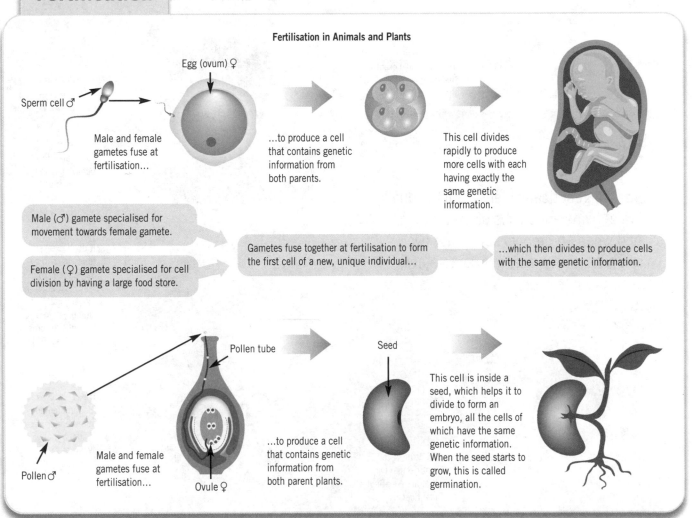

Fertilisation in Animals and Plants

Sperm cell ♂

Egg (ovum) ♀

Male and female gametes fuse at fertilisation...

...to produce a cell that contains genetic information from both parents.

This cell divides rapidly to produce more cells with each having exactly the same genetic information.

Male (♂) gamete specialised for movement towards female gamete.

Female (♀) gamete specialised for cell division by having a large food store.

Gametes fuse together at fertilisation to form the first cell of a new, unique individual...

...which then divides to produce cells with the same genetic information.

Pollen tube

Seed

Pollen ♂

Male and female gametes fuse at fertilisation...

Ovule ♀

...to produce a cell that contains genetic information from both parent plants.

This cell is inside a seed, which helps it to divide to form an embryo, all the cells of which have the same genetic information. When the seed starts to grow, this is called germination.

Variety in the Environment

Asexual Reproduction

Asexual reproduction...
- only needs one organism
- can produce other organisms without the need for genetic material from another individual.

A simple, single-celled animal like an amoeba can divide to produce new genetically identical offspring. Plants can also produce genetically identical offspring, for example, the spider plant.

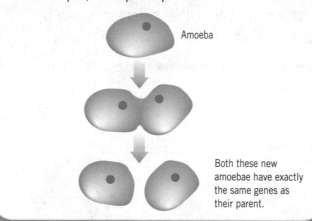

Amoeba

Both these new amoebae have exactly the same genes as their parent.

Cloning

Clones are genetically identical individuals. Identical twins are clones of each other, formed when an embryo splits into two. This is a relatively rare, but completely natural, event.

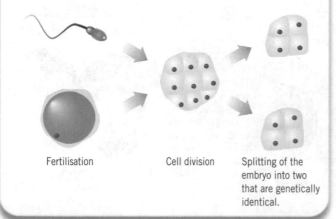

Fertilisation   Cell division   Splitting of the embryo into two that are genetically identical.

Artificial Cloning

In artificial cloning, steps are taken to ensure that all the genetic material comes from one parent:
- In gardening, a simple method is to take **cuttings** of a plant that you'd like to have lots of.

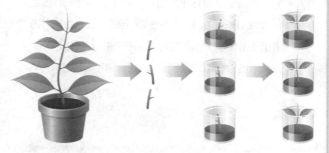

- With animals, the procedure is much more difficult.

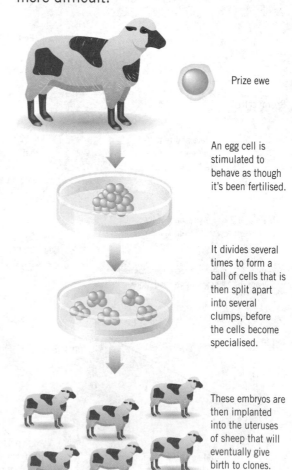

Prize ewe

An egg cell is stimulated to behave as though it's been fertilised.

It divides several times to form a ball of cells that is then split apart into several clumps, before the cells become specialised.

These embryos are then implanted into the uteruses of sheep that will eventually give birth to clones.

Competition Between Plants

Plants compete for space, light, water and minerals:

- If plants don't have enough space, they don't have room to grow.
- If they don't have enough light, they can't photosynthesise.
- If they don't have enough water, they will wilt and eventually die.

- If plants don't have enough minerals, they can't perform various chemical reactions, including photosynthesis. Nitrogen, potassium and phosphorus are the main minerals a plant needs. Nitrogen is used to help the plant make protein. Magnesium is also needed to make chlorophyll.

Plants can also be affected by animals and herbicides (chemicals that kill plants).

Use of Fertilisers

Fertilisers...

- can be bought in large bags and spread from the back of a tractor to provide all the necessary minerals a crop needs
- can be washed into rivers if too much is put on the fields.

Weeds

Weeds...

- are plants that aren't welcome in an area
- are 'wild' in the sense that they reproduce as best they can without man's help
- compete vigorously with other plants for space, light, water and minerals.

Use of Herbicides

Selective herbicides...

- can be sprayed onto crops in order to kill particular weeds without harming the food plant the farmer is growing
- remove a vital food resource for many small animals by killing the weeds. This can seriously affect other animals (and possibly the whole food web) by reducing the amount of food available. In some cases, this can result in animals eating more of the food crop to compensate.

In the food web opposite, the removal of weeds to increase growing space for the barley may remove a food source for the dormouse. This may result in the dormouse population having to eat more of the barley crop to survive. In addition, if the dormouse population declines, the fox and owl populations may also decline. This could result in more competition between foxes and hawks for rabbits.

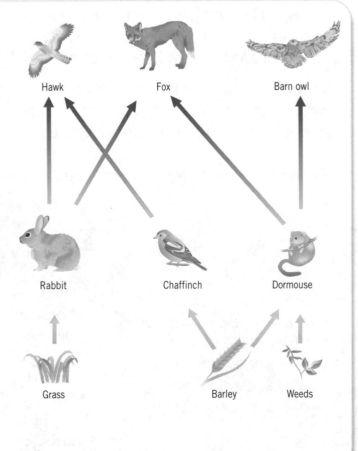

Hawk   Fox   Barn owl

Rabbit   Chaffinch   Dormouse

Grass   Barley   Weeds

Variety in the Environment

Competition Between Animals

Animals compete with each other for...
- food
- territory.

Territory is important as each animal needs a space that contains enough food for its survival. A territory also has to support enough animals to allow them to breed successfully.

Pests and Pesticides

Pests of plants...
- include field mice, caterpillars, aphids (greenfly), snails and slugs
- compete with humans for crops, and the more they eat, the fewer there are for humans.

Pesticides...
- are sprayed onto crops to kill animals that eat the crop plants
- improve the appearance of fruit and vegetables, which is extremely important to today's customers. If the food in the shop looks marked, it tends to get left on the shelf.

It's important to remember that each pest is part of a very complicated food web that can be affected by the removal of a certain species.

In addition, the pesticides aren't usually selective and kill useful insects and animals, as well as the pests. So, it might be better (and cheaper) to use a biological control, such as a predator insect to eat the pests, rather than a chemical pesticide.

Advantages of Using Pesticides	Disadvantages of Using Pesticides
<ul><li>Increases crop yield</li><li>Undamaged produce</li><li>Greater profitability</li></ul>	<ul><li>Effect on the food web</li><li>Accumulation of pesticides in the food web</li></ul>

Quick Test

1. What are gametes?
2. What is the name given to the time when a seed begins to grow?
3. What is a clone?
4. What is a selective herbicide?
5. What is a pesticide?
6. What is a biological control?

KEY WORDS

Make sure you understand these words before moving on!

- Asexual reproduction
- Biological control
- Cloning
- Crop yield
- Cuttings
- Gametes
- Herbicides
- Minerals
- Pesticides
- Selective
- Sexual reproduction
- Territory

Key Words Exercise

Match each key word with its meaning.

Key Word	Meaning
Asexual reproduction	Reproductive cells that fuse together at fertilisation
Biological control	Production of new individuals requiring male and female parents
Cloning	Production of new individuals requiring only one parent
Crop yield	Producing exact genetic copies of an organism
Cuttings	Small sections of a plant grown into separate copies in different places
Gametes	The amount of crop produced in a growing season
Herbicides	Using a living organism to keep pest numbers down in a crop
Minerals	Substances that are necessary for chemical reactions such as photosynthesis
Pesticides	Something that only affects certain types of plant or animal, not all of them
Selective	An area needed by animals to allow feeding and breeding
Sexual reproduction	Substances used to kill plants
Territory	Substances used to kill animals such as insects, slugs or other pests

Comprehension

Read the passage about strawberry plants, then answer the following questions.

1 Suggest how it's an advantage for the grower to plant strawberries through plastic sheeting?

2 a) What resources would the runners compete for in the strawberry plant?

   b) Why would this reduce the yield if they weren't removed?

3 The runners are clones of the parent. What does this mean?

4 The fungi are living organisms. What sort of pest control is this an example of?

Strawberries are grown commercially in raised rows in large fields. They're usually planted through holes in plastic sheeting that covers the soil. Irrigation tubes run under the plastic to carry water.

Later in the season, strawberry plants produce runners, as well as flowers for fruit. Runners are stem-like outgrowths along which small plantlets form. For the first two years or so, the runners are cut off because they compete with the flowers for resources in the plant and therefore reduce the yield. After a few years, though, the runners are potted up and allowed to root. Once rooted, the new plants are cut away from the parent plant and used to renew the growing stock.

Chafer grubs are pests of strawberry plants because they eat the roots. Pathogenic fungi are sometimes introduced into the soil when planting the strawberries because they attack and kill the grubs.

Variety in the Environment

1 **Fill in the missing words to complete the sentences about sexual and asexual reproduction.**

a) Sexual reproduction depends on the fusion of two _____, which are cells specialised for this job. In humans, they are the _____ and the _____, one of which is specialised for _____ and the other by having a large _____.

b) The moment of fusion is called _____, when the _____ from the two cells combine to form a genetically _____ individual. This new individual now carries _____ from both its _____ and, as a result, may have similar _____ to one or other of them.

c) Asexual reproduction doesn't depend on other individuals at all since only one _____ is involved. Plants are much better at this method of reproduction as only relatively few _____, such as amoebae, are capable of it.

d) The offspring produced by asexual reproduction are _____ and show no _____. Because of this, gardeners often produce more plants by taking _____, as they know the offspring will be exactly like the parent plants.

2 **Read this label from a container of weedkiller called Grassonly, then answer the questions.**

a) What is a selective weedkiller?

b) What do you think is the difference between the shape of grass and weed leaves?

c) Suggest two reasons why you would want to remove weeds from your lawn.

d) If you left large plants like buttercups in your lawn, what would happen to the grass?

e) Why would it be important to wear protective clothing when using Grassonly?

Selective weedkiller, for control of broadleaved weeds in lawns, such as dandelions, clover, buttercups and daisies. ACTIVE INGREDIENT = 2,4-D Poisonous if swallowed
- Do not spray on windy days.
- Use with caution and prevent spray contact with broadleaved shrubs close to lawn area.
- Wear protective clothing, especially gloves, when mixing and using solution.
- Do not dispose of unused chemical or solution into drains or watercourses.
- Wash hands after use.
- Store in a cool place and keep out of reach of small children.

GRASSONLY

Skills Practice

Some pupils set up an experiment in two plots in the school garden to investigate the effect of pesticide on the lettuce crop.

They planted each plot with the same amount of lettuce seeds and gave each plot the same amount of water each day.

After several weeks, when the plants were growing well, one plot was sprayed with a solution of a pesticide, the other sprayed with water.

Each day, the pupils went out and counted the number of caterpillars, slugs and snails that they could find.

Six weeks later, the pupils harvested their lettuces and weighed them. Their results are shown in the tables below.

Plot Sprayed with Water

Week	1	2	3	4	5	6
Number of caterpillars	4	10	14	20	22	8
Number of slugs	2	6	8	12	14	16
Number of snails	0	1	0	3	2	2

Plot Sprayed with Pesticide

Week	1	2	3	4	5	6
Number of caterpillars	0	0	4	10	12	2
Number of slugs	0	0	0	6	9	12
Number of snails	0	0	1	1	2	2

1. Plot the data in the form of two bar graphs, labelling the axes clearly.

2. What variables would the pupils have to assume would remain the same in order to make this investigation a fair test?

3. What is the dependent variable (the variable that's being measured) in this investigation?

4. Does the pesticide affect the pests? Give a reason for your answer.

5. In the end, the water-sprayed plot produced 2450g of lettuce and the pesticide-sprayed plot produced 3020g. Does the pesticide affect the yield? Give a reason for your answer.

6. The numbers of pests went up in both plots almost each week. Why do you think this happened?

7. Suggest a reason why the number of caterpillars dropped in week 6.

The Reactivity of Metals

The Changing Appearance of Metals

Over time, many metals are affected by air and water. Different metals are affected in different ways and some examples are shown in the table opposite.

Gold objects don't react at all; gold is described as being unreactive.

Most metals are hard but a few, like lithium (Li), sodium (Na) and potassium (K), are much softer and can be cut with a sharp knife. These three metals are found in group 1 of the periodic table. This group is known as the alkali metals.

Alkali metals...
- are shiny when freshly cut
- **tarnish** (become dull) very quickly when exposed to air.

Metal	Example Object	How the Object Changes Over Time
Iron	Nail	It **rusts**
Silver	Ring	It becomes dull
Copper	Water pipe	It gets darker
Aluminium	Aluminium can	It goes grey

The Reactivity Series

You can place metals into an order of reactivity by analysing how they react with water, oxygen or acid. This enables you to arrange metals from the most reactive to the least reactive in a **reactivity series**.

The order of reactivity for the metals is the same whether water, oxygen or acid is used, and whichever acid is used.

The diagram opposite shows a sample of metal placed in acid. The rate of reaction can be judged by...
- counting the number of bubbles of gas released
- measuring the temperature change using a thermometer.

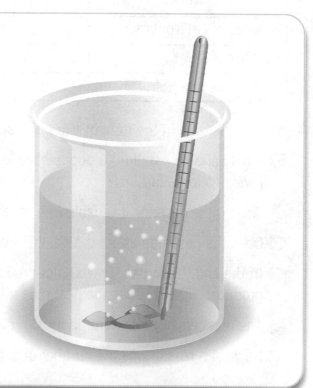

Reactions of Metals with Water

Some metals react with cold water to form metal hydroxides (or metal oxides) and hydrogen gas. Metal hydroxide solutions are **alkaline** and have a pH above 7.

Lithium, sodium and potassium all float on water. This shows they're less dense than water. These metals react **vigorously** (quickly) with water:

- The hydrogen released when sodium reacts with water can be lit using a lighted splint.
- Potassium reacts so vigorously that the hydrogen released burns readily.
- Lithium, sodium and potassium are all stored in oil to stop them reacting with oxygen or moisture in the air.

Sodium is one of the metals that reacts with cold water:

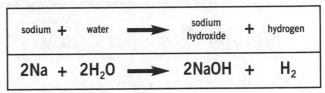

$$2Na + 2H_2O \longrightarrow 2NaOH + H_2$$

The experiment above can be carried out safely in the laboratory if...

- the teacher carries out the experiment as a demonstration
- the teacher wears goggles
- only very small pieces of metal are used
- a safety screen is used to protect people observing the reaction.

Copper doesn't react with water, while iron and calcium only react slowly.

How Metals React Differently with Water

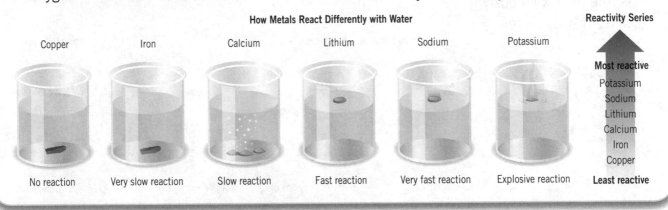

Copper	Iron	Calcium	Lithium	Sodium	Potassium
No reaction	Very slow reaction	Slow reaction	Fast reaction	Very fast reaction	Explosive reaction

Reactivity Series

Most reactive
Potassium
Sodium
Lithium
Calcium
Iron
Copper
Least reactive

Reactions of Metals with Acids

You'll remember that some metals react with acids to form a salt and hydrogen:

The more reactive the metal, the more bubbles are seen and the higher the temperature rise. The same amount of acid and the same amount of metal should be used to make this a fair test.

How Metals React Differently with Acids

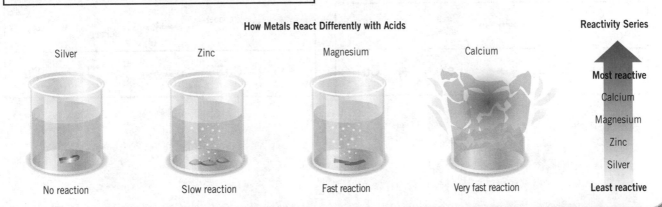

Silver	Zinc	Magnesium	Calcium
No reaction	Slow reaction	Fast reaction	Very fast reaction

Reactivity Series

Most reactive
Calcium
Magnesium
Zinc
Silver
Least reactive

The Reactivity of Metals

Reactions of Metals with Oxygen

Some metals react with oxygen to form metal oxides:

metal + oxygen ⟶ metal oxide

Metals react with oxygen in the following ways:
- When metals are burned in air, they react with the oxygen.
- If a metal is burned in pure oxygen, the reaction is much more vigorous.
- The higher up the reactivity series a metal is, the more vigorously it will be expected to react with oxygen.

- Heating a metal using a Bunsen burner speeds up the rate at which it reacts with oxygen.

It's very important to work safely in the laboratory. When using a Bunsen burner to heat the metals...
- long hair should be tied back
- goggles must be worn
- tongs must be used to hold the metal
- avoid looking directly at burning magnesium.

How Metals React Differently with Oxygen

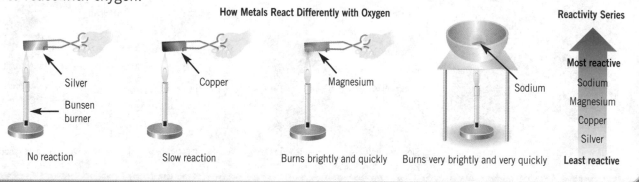

Silver — Bunsen burner — No reaction

Copper — Slow reaction

Magnesium — Burns brightly and quickly

Sodium — Burns very brightly and very quickly

Reactivity Series

Most reactive
Sodium
Magnesium
Copper
Silver
Least reactive

Displacement Reactions

A more reactive metal **displaces** a less reactive metal from its compound. Iron is more reactive than copper, so iron displaces copper from a solution of copper sulfate.

iron	+	copper sulfate	⟶	iron sulfate	+	copper

$$Fe + CuSO_4 \longrightarrow FeSO_4 + Cu$$

You can use the reactivity series to predict displacement reactions. Zinc is more reactive than copper, so you can predict that zinc will displace copper from a solution of copper sulfate.

zinc	+	copper sulfate	⟶	zinc sulfate	+	copper

$$Zn + CuSO_4 \longrightarrow ZnSO_4 + Cu$$

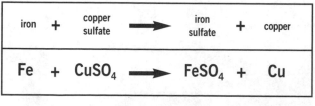

Blue copper sulfate solution

Iron nail is put in

Displacement reaction takes place

Iron nail is pulled out

Green iron sulfate solution

Copper

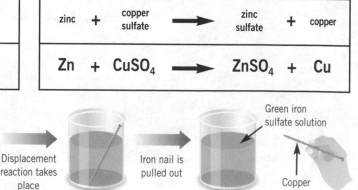

Useful Displacement Reactions

Displacement reactions can be very useful in everyday life. For example, broken iron railway tracks can be mended using **molten** (liquid) iron. The iron is produced using the displacement reaction between iron (III) oxide and aluminium:

- Aluminium is more reactive than iron, so it displaces iron from iron oxide.
- So much heat is released by the reaction that the iron is molten, which means it can be poured directly into the gaps in the tracks.
- This is known as a thermite reaction.

Extracting Metals

Copper and gold were the first metals known and used by people. They're very unreactive:
- Gold is found uncombined in nature.
- Most copper is found in compounds in rocks; it can be easily extracted from these compounds by heating the rocks in the presence of carbon.

Very reactive metals, like sodium and potassium, are only found in compounds. These metals...
- are difficult to extract from their compounds; normally they're extracted using electricity
- were discovered much more recently.

Using Metals

The way that a metal is used depends on its properties and how reactive it is.
Copper is used...
- to make water pipes because it has low reactivity
- in electrical wiring because it's a good **electrical conductor**
- to make saucepans because it's a good **thermal conductor**.

Aluminium has a low density and is much less reactive than might be expected because it reacts with oxygen to form a layer of aluminium oxide, which stops any further reaction.
Aluminium is used to...
- form aluminium alloys, which are used to make aircraft because they have a low density
- make greenhouse frames because the layer of aluminium oxide stops any further reaction.

Quick Test

1. Name a metal that doesn't tarnish, even over very long periods of time.
2. Which solution is alkaline: solution A (pH 7); solution B (pH 3); solution C (pH 10)?
3. Name the compound formed when copper reacts with oxygen.
4. Complete this equation:
   copper sulfate + iron ⟶ _____ + _____

KEY WORDS
Make sure you understand these words before moving on!
- Alkaline
- Displaces
- Electrical conductor
- Molten
- Reactivity series
- Rust
- Tarnish
- Thermal conductor
- Vigorously

The Reactivity of Metals

Key Words Exercise

Match each key word with its meaning.

Key Word		Meaning
Alkaline		A material that electricity can pass through easily
Displaces		A solution that has a pH greater than 7
Electrical conductor		Quickly
Molten		A list that places the metals in order from the most reactive to the least reactive
Reactivity series		A compound formed when iron reacts with oxygen and water
Rust		Liquid
Tarnish		Become dull
Thermal conductor		A material that heat can pass through easily
Vigorously		Takes the place of

Comprehension

Read the passage about rusting, then answer the following questions.

1. What is an alloy?

2. Why do different steels have different properties?

3. a) Why is stainless steel a very useful alloy?
   b) How is stainless steel used?

4. What is the chemical name for rust?

5. Why does a layer of paint prevent iron from rusting?

Iron is usually turned into an alloy. Alloys are mixtures of metals. The most common alloy of iron is called steel. Different types of steel can be made by using different types of metals in different proportions. The different steels have different properties.

The type of steel selected for a particular application will depend on the properties required. Stainless steel is made by mixing iron and chromium. It's very resistant to corrosion and is widely used to make cutlery and saucepans.

If iron or iron alloys are exposed to water and oxygen, they will eventually react to form hydrated iron oxide (rust). Even stainless steel will eventually rust. Many other metals also react to form metal oxides, but these metal oxides aren't referred to as rust.

Iron can be protected from rusting by coating the metal with a layer of plastic, paint or oil. This stops the oxygen and water from reaching the metal. But if the coating is scratched, the iron will start to rust. Iron can also be protected from rusting by placing it in contact with a more reactive metal, such as magnesium. The more reactive metal reacts, leaving the iron intact.

Testing Understanding

1 **Fill in the missing words to complete the sentences about the reactivity of metals.**

a) Over time, the appearance of many metals changes as they're affected by

_____ and _____. Silver objects become

_____ and iron objects _____. But gold objects remain

the same because gold is a very _____ metal.

b) Magnesium is a fairly reactive metal. It reacts with hydrochloric acid to form a salt called

_____ _____ and hydrogen gas.

c) When metals are heated, they react with _____ in the air to form metal

_____. By observing the reaction between metals and oxygen, you can place

the metals into an order of reactivity from the most to the _____ reactive.

d) In displacement reactions, a _____ reactive metal displaces a

_____ reactive metal from its compound. In the reaction between iron

and copper sulfate, the iron, which is _____ reactive, displaces the

copper to form _____ and _____.

2 **Read the information provided, then answer the questions that follow.**

Andy wanted to investigate what happened when different metals were placed in dilute acid. He measured 10cm^3 of acid and then placed it into a boiling tube. He measured the temperature of the acid. He then placed a piece of zinc into the acid and measured the new temperature.

Metal Used	Temp. at Start (°C)	Temp. at End (°C)	Temp. Change (°C)
Zinc	21	23	
Copper	21	21	
Magnesium	20	23	

Andy repeated the experiment using copper and magnesium metals.

a) Name the piece of equipment that Andy could use to measure the temperature.

b) Name the piece of equipment that Andy could use to measure the volume of acid.

c) Copy and complete the table above right to show the temperature change for each metal.

d) Copy and complete the axes opposite, and show the results of Andy's experiment as a bar graph.

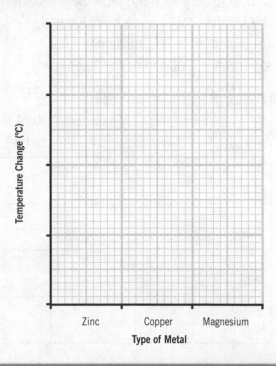

The Reactivity of Metals

Pauline wants to investigate the reactivity of different metals by measuring the temperature rise when they're placed in dilute acid. Her experiment is illustrated below.

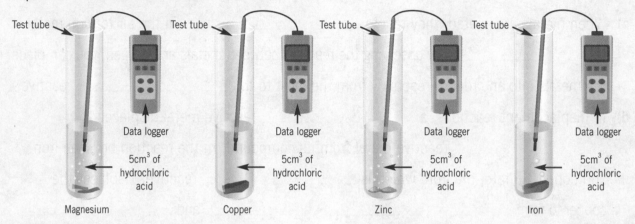

Test tube   Test tube   Test tube   Test tube

Data logger   Data logger   Data logger   Data logger

5cm³ of   5cm³ of   5cm³ of   5cm³ of
hydrochloric   hydrochloric   hydrochloric   hydrochloric
acid   acid   acid   acid

Magnesium   Copper   Zinc   Iron

1 a) Pauline uses a data logger to measure the temperature rise in her experiments. Suggest another piece of apparatus that Pauline could use to measure the temperature change.

b) Suggest one advantage of using a data logger.

2 Copy and complete the table below to show the factors that Pauline has changed, measured and kept the same in her experiment. Put one tick in each row.

Factor	Is it Changed?	Is it Measured?	Is it Kept the Same?
Volume of acid			
Type of metal			
Type of acid			
Temp. rise			

Pauline's results are in the table below.

Type of Metal	Temperature Rise (°C)
Magnesium	5
Copper	0
Zinc	2
Iron	1

3 Copy the axes below and show the results of Pauline's experiment as a bar graph.

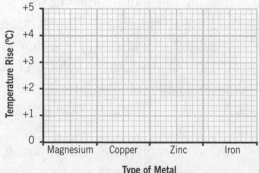

4 Put the metals in this experiment into an order of reactivity. Place the most reactive metal first.

Pushing and Turning

Pushing Forces

When a force pushes on a surface, it causes **pressure**. The amount of pressure depends on…
* the size of the force applied
* the area that the force is acting on.

If a force is spread over a larger area, the pressure is less. If a force is concentrated on a smaller area, the pressure is greater.

For example, the pressure caused by a woman treading on your toe wearing trainers would be less (and it would hurt less!) than the same woman treading on your toe if she was wearing stiletto heels. This is because, although the size of the force is the same, the area of the stiletto heel is much smaller.

Increasing Pressure

The following examples show how pressure can be increased by reducing the area over which a force acts:
* Studs on football boots provide better grip.
* A knife has a sharp edge with a very small area, allowing it to cut easily.
* When you push a drawing pin, the force is spread over the area of the head of the pin. The same force is concentrated over the much smaller area of the pin point, creating much more pressure. As a result, the pin sticks into the notice board, not into your finger.

Pushing and Turning

Decreasing Pressure

The following examples show how pressure can be decreased by increasing the area over which a force acts:

- Snow shoes have a large area to stop the person wearing them sinking into the snow.
- Camels' feet have a large area to prevent them from sinking into the sand.

Calculating Pressure

The pressure exerted by a force is calculated by:

$$\text{pressure} = \frac{\text{force}}{\text{area}}$$

The unit of pressure is newtons per square metre (N/m^2) or newtons per square centimetre (N/cm^2).

For example, you could calculate the pressure exerted by a metal cube of weight 500N with dimensions 10cm × 10cm × 10cm:

$$\text{pressure} = \frac{\text{force}}{\text{area}} = \frac{500N}{100cm^2} = 5N/cm^2$$

Pressure in Gases

Gases exert pressure as the gas particles **collide** with the walls of the container they're in.

The gas particles inside a balloon exert pressure on the walls of the balloon. This allows the balloon to hold its shape.

There are different ways of increasing the pressure in a gas:

- Increase the number of gas particles in a container of fixed volume. This means the particles collide with the walls more frequently.
- Reduce the volume of the container for a fixed number of gas particles. This means the particles collide with the walls more frequently.
- Increase the temperature of the gas to give the particles more kinetic energy. This means they collide with the walls more frequently and with a greater force.

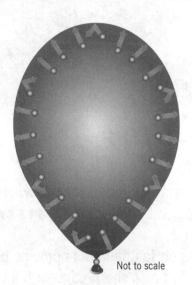

Not to scale

The air around you is at **atmospheric** pressure:

- Normal atmospheric pressure is $101\,000N/m^2$.
- The atmosphere doesn't crush you because the pressure of the blood in your body is strong enough to balance the atmospheric pressure.

Pressure in Liquids

Unlike gases, liquids can't be compressed. But liquids can transmit pressure. **Hydraulic** systems use liquids to transmit pressure:

- Hydraulic brakes in a car use fluid to transmit pressure from the foot pedal to the brake pads.
- If an air bubble gets into the brake fluid, it can stop the transmission of the pressure, so the brakes may not work properly.

The pressure in liquids increases with depth:

- The pressure at the bottom of the ocean is very high because of the weight of the water pushing down. Deep-sea submarines and creatures that live at the bottom of the oceans must be able to withstand very high pressures.
- **Dams** are wider at the base because this is where the pressure of the water is greatest.

Increasing pressure

Turning Forces

A force can turn an object around a hinge or **pivot**. A **fulcrum** is another name for a hinge or pivot.

When you open a door, you're using a turning force. The door turns around the hinges. This turning force is known as the **moment** of the force.

The moment of a force depends on...
- the size of the force
- the distance between the force and the pivot.

A greater distance between the force and the pivot increases the moment of the force.

A door handle is as far away as possible from the hinges in order to increase the moment of the force. If the handle was close to the hinges, it would be difficult to open the door.

Other everyday objects also use the principle of moments:

- A spanner provides a moment to undo a nut. A spanner with a longer handle increases the moment of the force and can undo a tighter nut.
- A **lever** can be used to lift a heavy load or open a can of paint. Increasing the length of the lever increases the moment of the force.
- The wheel of a wheelbarrow acts as a pivot. The handles are placed as far away as possible from the wheel in order to increase the moment and make it easier to lift the load.

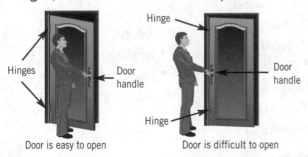

Hinge

Hinges

Door handle

Door handle

Hinge

Door is easy to open

Door is difficult to open

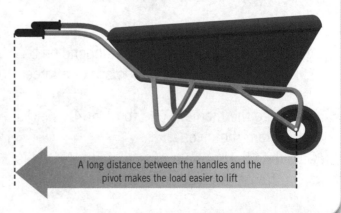

A long distance between the handles and the pivot makes the load easier to lift

Pushing and Turning

Balancing Moments

The two children on the seesaw below are **balanced**. The boy has a greater weight than the girl, but he is closer to the pivot.

It's possible to calculate the moment of each child using the following equation:

the moment of a force $=$ force $\times$ distance from the pivot

The moment of the force created by the boy is equal to 900N x 2.0m = 1800Nm.

The moment of the force created by the girl is equal to 600N x 3.0m = 1800Nm.

The moments of the forces on each side of the seesaw are equal, so the seesaw balances.

600N

900N

3m

2m

Pivot

Quick Test

1. What is the unit of pressure?
2. What two things does pressure depend on?
3. What two things does the moment of a force depend on?
4. Calculate the moment of a force of 4N that is 2.5m from the pivot.
5. Calculate the moment of a force of 4N that is 1.5m from the pivot.

Key Words Exercise

Match each key word to its meaning.

Key Word	Meaning
Atmospheric	This is equal to force / area
Balanced	The turning effect of a force
Collide	The point from which a turning force acts
Dam	Another word for pivot
Fulcrum	The pressure of the air around us
Hydraulic	This is how gas particles exert pressure on the walls of a container
Lever	A system that transmits pressure through a liquid
Moment	When the moments of the forces are equal
Pivot	This uses the principle of moments to lift a heavy load
Pressure	This is wider at the bottom because of the increase in the pressure of the water at a greater depth

Comprehension

Read the passage about levers, then answer the following questions.

1. Explain the connection between the word 'lever' and its original meaning in French.

2. Give four examples of levers that people regularly use.

3. What feature of levers allowed Archimedes to claim that he could use a lever to move the whole world?

4. Suggest why many historians believe that the ancient Egyptians used levers.

The word lever comes from the French word 'lever', which means 'to lift'. A lever uses a pivot to multiply a force applied to an object. You may not realise it, but levers are everywhere. The average person uses a lever many times each day. Imagine life without door handles, staplers, bike gears, car jacks, can openers and scissors. Almost every moveable joint is connected to a lever.

The ancient Greek, Archimedes, was the first to explain levers, describing a relationship between the force and the distance from the pivot. He once famously said 'Give me a lever long enough and a fulcrum on which to place it, and I shall move the world'. Many historians believe that ancient Egyptian construction techniques involved levers. This could explain how they managed to move the huge stone blocks they used to build the pyramids.

Pushing and Turning

1 **Fill in the missing words to complete the sentences about pushing and turning.**

a) If a _____ is spread over a larger area, the _____ is less.

If a force is concentrated on a smaller _____, the pressure is greater.

b) Pressure can be _____ by decreasing the area on which a force acts.

_____ on football boots increase the pressure because

_____ area is in contact with the _____ compared with

a normal trainer. This is why they give more grip. A _____ has a sharp

edge with a very small area, allowing it to cut easily.

c) Pressure can be decreased by _____ the area over which a force acts.

Snow shoes have a large area to _____ the pressure, preventing the

wearer from _____ into the snow. _____ feet have a

large area that decreases the pressure, preventing them from sinking into the sand.

2 **Look at the diagram below of two children sitting on a seesaw.**

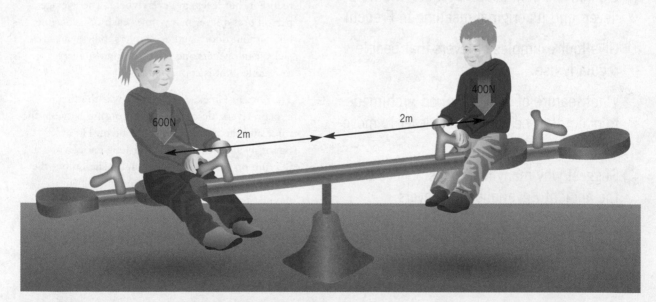

a) Calculate the moment created by the girl.

b) Calculate the moment created by the boy.

c) Explain why the seesaw isn't balanced.

d) Explain how the seesaw could be made to balance by moving the position of one of the children.

ESSENTIALS

Year 9
KS3 Science
Coursebook Answers

DISRUPTION OF LIFE PROCESSES

Page 7 – Quick Test

1. A disease-causing microbe

2. Bacteria, viruses and fungi

3. Nicotine

4. Alveoli

5. Liver and brain

6. Antibodies

Page 8 – Key Words Exercise

Alveoli – The air sacs where oxygen enters and carbon dioxide leaves the blood

Antibodies – Substances produced by white blood cells that can neutralise a specific microbe

Antitoxins – Chemicals that neutralise a poison produced by a microbe

Bronchitis – A condition in which air sacs are damaged due to constant coughing

Emphysema – A smoking-related disease caused by excessive mucus and smoke particles

Hallucinogens – Substances that cause hallucinations

Immunity – Protection from disease by the production of antibodies

Nicotine – An addictive chemical found in cigarette smoke

Pathogen – A disease-causing microbe

Vaccine – A collection of dead or weakened microbes, or antibodies, injected to give protection

Page 8 – Comprehension

1. **Any sensible answer, e.g.:** by using smoking by well-known celebrities, or in places that are well known, to make it appear a 'good' thing.

2. The groups should have had equal numbers of people; the people should have been of the same ages; the people should have had similar builds/lifestyles; there should have been the same numbers of males and females.

3. The study showed that smoking led to an increase in the likelihood of contracting lung cancer, so it could have put people off buying cigarettes.

4. Not true – it only increases the chances of getting lung cancer.

Page 9 – Testing Understanding

1. a) **In any order:** bacteria; viruses; fungi

   b) bacteria; viruses; fungi

   c) white blood; antitoxins; antibodies; stick / attach; digest

   d) immunisation / vaccination; dead / killed; antibodies

   e) alcohol; drugs; addicted

2. a)
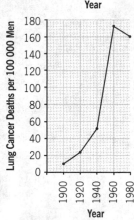

   b) The number of cigarettes smoked per year rose steeply until 1940 and then began to drop.

   c) The number of deaths rose until 1960 and then began to drop.

Page 10 – Skills Practice

1. **Any one from:** they could measure the diameter of each area with a ruler; they could measure the area of each by putting it over graph paper and counting the squares.

2. C as it had the biggest clear area.

3. As a control to show that it was the penicillin, not the liquid-soaked disc, that caused the effect.

4. They were using bacteria that could have harmed them.

5. To kill any harmful bacteria on their hands / to prevent contamination from their hands.

METALS AND METAL COMPOUNDS

Page 14 – Quick Test

1. Hydrogen

2. Zinc sulfate

3. Sodium chloride

4. Copper nitrate

5. Alkali + acid → salt + water

Page 15 – Key Words Exercise

Acid – The chemical opposite of bases; these compounds all contain the element hydrogen

Alkali – A soluble base

Carbon dioxide – A gas, produced when a metal carbonate reacts with an acid, which turns limewater cloudy

Element – A substance that's made of only one type of atom

Evaporates – Turns from a liquid to a gas

Formula – A way of representing the type and number of atoms in the smallest particle of a substance

Hydrogen – A gas, produced when a metal reacts with an acid, which burns with a squeaky pop

Insoluble – Doesn't dissolve

Metal carbonate – A chemical compound that contains metal, carbon and oxygen atoms

Symbol – A one or two-letter code used to represent an element

Page 15 – Comprehension

1. Sodium chloride

2. Breakfast cereals; ready-made sandwiches; pasta sauces

3. 6g

4. Less than 6g

5. 50 000

6. Stroke; heart disease; eye damage; kidney damage

Page 16 – Testing Understanding

1. a) good; graphite

   b) type; two; one; four

   c) hydrogen; squeaky; nitrate

   d) salt; limewater

   e) water; chloride; gas

2. a) iron chloride; hydrogen

   b) Bubble it through limewater and it turns the limewater cloudy.

   c)
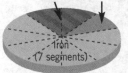

Page 17 – Skills Practice

1.

Test Tube	Any Water?	Any Oxygen?
1	No	Yes
2	Yes	No
3	Yes	Yes

2. The iron nail only rusts when water and oxygen are present.

3. There would be little or no rust because the layer of oil stops the water and oxygen from reaching the iron nail.

ENERGY AND ELECTRICITY

Page 21 – Quick Test

1. **Any three from:** the wind; the Sun; water in rivers and reservoirs; tides in the sea

2. **Any three from:** in fuels; in batteries; in our bodies; in food

3. Volts

4. Direct current / current that flows in one direction.

5. Alternating current / current that changes direction.

Page 22 – Key Words Exercise

Alternating current – Current that continuously changes direction, created by a generator

Brushes – These ensure continuous contact of the wires in a generator as the coil rotates

Device – Something that transfers energy from one form to another

Direct current – Current supplied by a cell or battery

Double insulated – A device with a plastic casing

Generator – A coil of wire rotating between the poles of a magnet

Mains electricity – This electricity comes to your home at 230–240V

National Grid – A network of cables taking electricity from power stations to homes

Potential difference – This tells you how much energy is transferred in a cell or in a bulb in an electric circuit

Substations – The parts of the National Grid that contain step-up or step-down transformers

Transformer – This changes the voltage to a safer level for use in homes

Turbine – This usually drives a generator in a power station

Page 22 – Comprehension

1. It can increase the greenhouse effect and lead to global warming.

2. They change the landscape; they can disturb wildlife; they only produce a small amount of electricity.

3. a) **Any one from:** it releases no harmful gases into the atmosphere; it's a very efficient way of producing electricity.

   b) **Any one from:** waste material can be expensive to dispose of safely; the risk of accidental emission of radioactive material.

Page 23 – Testing Understanding

1. a) power stations; cables; National Grid; pylons; high

b) electricity; homes; current; less; heat

c) step-down; substations; safer; mains

2. a)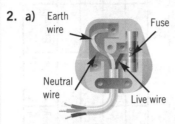
Earth wire
Fuse
Neutral wire
Live wire

b) The live wire controls the AC current, flowing backwards and forwards many times per second. The neutral wire completes the circuit.

c) Devices that are cased in plastic. Because plastic is an electrical insulator, this adds another layer of insulation to the device – hence the name double insulation.

d) The earth wire

Page 24 – Skills Practice

1.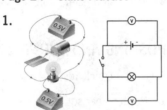

2. The amount of energy transferred in the bulb from the current to heat and light.

3. They should read the same value.

4. This shows that energy is conserved in the circuit.

5.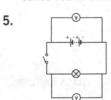

6. Both values will increase. If the second cell is identical to the first, both values will double.

VARIETY IN THE ENVIRONMENT

Page 28 – Quick Test

1. Sex cells

2. Germination

3. An individual that is genetically identical to another.

4. A chemical that kills only certain plants.

5. A chemical that kills pests.

6. The use of one organism to control the numbers of another.

Page 29 – Key Words Exercise

Asexual reproduction – Production of new individuals requiring only one parent

Biological control – Using a living organism to keep pest numbers down in a crop

Cloning – Producing exact genetic copies of an organism

Crop yield – The amount of crop produced in a growing season

Cuttings – Small sections of a plant grown into separate copies in different places

Gametes – Reproductive cells that fuse together at fertilisation

Herbicides – Substances used to kill plants

Minerals – Substances that are necessary for chemical reactions such as photosynthesis

Pesticides – Substances used to kill animals such as insects, slugs or other pests

Selective – Something that only affects certain types of plant or animal, not all of them

Sexual reproduction – Production of new individuals requiring male and female parents

Territory – An area needed by animals to allow feeding and breeding

Page 29 – Comprehension

1. To prevent weeds from growing and competing with the strawberries.

2. a) Water and minerals / nutrients

   b) Fewer resources would get to the flowers / fruit, so there would be less fruit.

3. They're genetically identical to the parent.

4. Biological control

Page 30 – Testing Understanding

1. a) gametes; sperm / eggs; eggs / sperm; moving / movement; food store

   b) fertilisation; nuclei; unique; genes / chromosomes / DNA; parents; characteristics / traits

   c) parent / individual / organism; animals

   d) identical; differences; cuttings

2. a) A weedkiller that only kills certain plants / types of plant.

   b) **Any one from:** weed leaves are broader than grass leaves; grass leaves are narrower than weed leaves.

   c) To improve the appearance of the lawn; to remove plants that are competing with the grass / to keep only grass plants in the lawn.

   d) The grass could disappear as buttercups would outcompete it for resources, especially light.

   e) It's harmful / poisonous to us.

Page 31 – Skills Practice

1.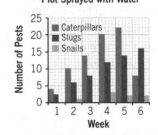

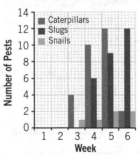

2. Temperature; soil pH; the amount of light; the amount of nutrient in the soil

3. The number of pests

4. Yes. The numbers of pests were lower in each case, although there was little difference in snail numbers.

5. Yes. The amounts were quite different provided that all other factors were the same (for example, none of the lettuces in the water-sprayed plot were eaten by other animals / birds, etc).

6. The lettuces got bigger, so there was more food available.

7. **Any one from:** they got eaten by birds / other animals; they were killed by a disease; they hatched into butterflies after week 5.

THE REACTIVITY OF METALS

Page 35 – Quick Test

1. **Any sensible answer, e.g.:** gold

2. Solution C

3. Copper oxide

4. iron sulfate; copper

Page 36 – Key Words Exercise

Alkaline – A solution that has a pH greater than 7
Displaces – Takes the place of
Electrical conductor – A material that electricity can pass through easily
Molten – Liquid
Reactivity series – A list that places the metals in order from the most reactive to the least reactive
Rust – A compound formed when iron reacts with oxygen and water
Tarnish – Become dull
Thermal conductor – A material that heat can pass through easily
Vigorously – Quickly

Page 36 – Comprehension

1. A mixture of metals

2. They are made from different metals in different proportions.

3. a) It's very resistant to corrosion.
   b) To make cutlery and saucepans.

4. Hydrated iron oxide

5. It stops the oxygen and water from reaching the iron.

Page 37 – Testing Understanding

1. a) air / water; water / air; dull; rust; unreactive
   b) magnesium chloride
   c) oxygen; oxides; least
   d) more; less; more; iron sulfate; copper

2. a) **Any one from:** a thermometer; a data logger
   b) A measuring cylinder
   c)

Metal Used	Temp. at Start (°C)	Temp. at End (°C)	Temp. Change (°C)
Zinc	21	23	2
Copper	21	21	0
Magnesium	20	23	3

   d)

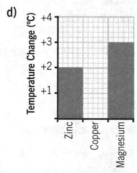

Type of Metal

Page 38 – Skills Practice

1. a) A thermometer
   b) **Any one from:** it logs the results; it's more accurate / precise; it measures more temperature points over time.

2.

Factor	Is it Changed?	Is it Measured?	Is it Kept the Same?
Volume of acid			✓
Type of metal	✓		
Type of acid			✓
Temp. rise		✓	

3.

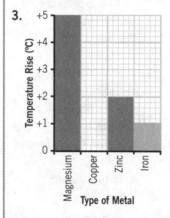

Type of Metal

4. Magnesium, zinc, iron, copper

PUSHING AND TURNING

Page 42 – Quick Test

1. Newtons per square metre (N/m^2) or newtons per square centimetre (N/cm^2)

2. The size of the force applied and the area that the force is acting on.

3. The size of the force and the distance from the force to the pivot.

4. 10Nm

5. 6Nm

Page 43 – Key Words Exercise

Atmospheric – The pressure of the air around us
Balanced – When the moments of the forces are equal
Collide – This is how gas particles exert pressure on the walls of a container
Dam – This is wider at the bottom because of the increase in the pressure of the water at a greater depth
Fulcrum – Another word for pivot

Hydraulic – A system that transmits pressure through a liquid
Lever – This uses the principle of moments to lift a heavy load
Moment – The turning effect of a force
Pivot – The point from which a turning force acts
Pressure – This is equal to force / area

Page 43 – Comprehension

1. Lever means 'to lift' in French and levers are often used to lift things.

2. **Any sensible answers, e.g.:** door handles; staplers; bike gears; car jacks

3. If a lever was long enough, he would be able to produce a large enough force.

4. The huge stone blocks are very heavy and would have been very difficult to move. Levers would have made them easier to move.

Page 44 – Testing Understanding

1. a) force; pressure; area
   b) increased; Studs; less; ground; knife
   c) increasing; reduce; sinking; Camels'

2. a) 1200Nm
   b) 800Nm
   c) The moments aren't the same.
   d) The boy should be moved so he is 3.0m from the pivot.

Page 45 – Skills Practice

1. The temperature of the gas would be much hotter at the bottom if heated directly. The water allows the heat to be distributed more evenly.

2. **Any sensible answer up to a maximum of 2 minutes, e.g.:** Every 30s

3.

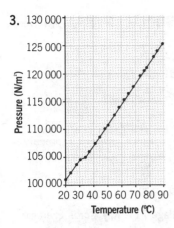

4. As the temperature of the gas increases, the pressure increases. They're proportional.

MANIPULATING THE ENVIRONMENT

Page 49 – Quick Test

1. Breeding for a desired characteristic.

2. The loss of a gene from a population.

3. Carbon dioxide

4. Oxygen

5. Because so much energy is lost at each step.

6. A genetically modified organism

Page 50 – Key Words Exercise

Bioaccumulation – An increase in the concentration of something along a food chain
Embryonic – Originating from the developing fertilised egg
Eutrophication – Caused by fertilisers in water, leading to stagnation
Global warming – An increase in the Earth's temperature caused by the thickening of the layer of carbon dioxide in the atmosphere
GMO – An organism that has had its genetic make-up artificially altered
Limiting factors – Environmental changes that alter a reaction like photosynthesis
Selective breeding – Using variation to breed a desired characteristic into the offspring
Stem cell – A cell able to develop into many different types

Sustainable development – Meeting human needs without damaging the environment
Varieties – A range of different types within the same species

Page 50 – Comprehension

1. Able to be broken down / decayed / decomposed in the soil.

2. To allow the microorganisms of decay / decomposition to respire.

3. The compost contains the broken down products from the decomposed plants.

4. They would slow / stop photosynthesis.

5. Organic cabbages are likely to be a little more 'eaten' in appearance / have holes in the leaves / be different sizes rather than a uniform size.

Page 51 – Testing Understanding

1. a) yield
   b) pests; vegetables; greenfly / blackfly
   c) food; insects; food; reduced / lessened; slugs; fewer; more
   d) Pesticides; diluted; concentrated; kill; bioaccumulation

2. a)

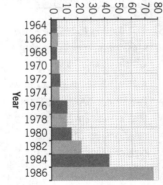

   b) **Any one from:** 59; 60 **(not 59.5).**
   c) 1983
   d) 12
   e) The small mammals ate insects, so the DDT accumulated in their bodies. The peregrines then ate lots of mammals (bioaccumulation).

Page 52 – Skills Practice

1.

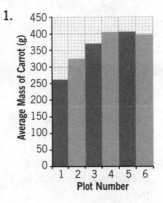

2. Up to 12g made a difference but this was probably the most that the carrots could take up from the soil, so the extra had no effect.

3. It could wash out into streams and rivers and cause pollution / eutrophication.

4. The mass of the carrots

5. The size of the plots; the amount of water / light; the number of seeds / plants planted; the amount of nutrient in the plot before the experiment; the amount of weeding.

ENVIRONMENTAL CHEMISTRY

Page 56 – Quick Test

1. A dark, sticky material, consisting of the remains of dead plants and animals, that holds pieces of rock together.

2. Add manure – as it rots down, acidic compounds are released.

3. Because carbon dioxide dissolves in it.

4. When sulfur oxides or nitrogen oxides dissolve in water.

5. **Any sensible answer, e.g.:** by lightning strikes

6. **Any sensible answers, e.g.:** methane; carbon dioxide

Page 57 – Key Words Exercise

Acid rain – A type of rain formed in polluted areas when sulfur oxides or nitrogen oxides dissolve in water
Carbonic acid – A chemical, formed when carbon dioxide dissolves in water, which makes normal rainwater slightly acidic
Deforestation – The cutting down of large numbers of trees
Fossil fuels – Non-renewable energy resources, such as coal, oil and natural gas, formed from plants and animals that lived long ago
Fungi – A type of microbe that decomposes plant and animal material
Greenhouse effect – How gases, including carbon dioxide and methane, cause the Earth to warm up
Humus – Dark, sticky material formed when plant and animal matter rots
Neutralisation – The reaction between an acid and an alkali
pH – A scale used to measure how acidic or alkaline something is
Quicklime – Calcium hydroxide
Satellite – An object that orbits a larger body
Sulfur dioxide – A toxic gas formed when sulfur is burned
Weathered – When a rock is broken down into smaller pieces

Page 57 – Comprehension

1. Spiders and insects

2. They're used to make some sunscreens and antibiotics.

3. A partnership where both partners benefit by the presence of the other.

4. The alga photosynthesises to provide food while the fungus provides a home for both plants.

5. That the level of air pollution is increasing.

Page 58 – Testing Understanding

1. a) pH; alkaline; acidic; quicklime; alkaline; lower
   b) carbon; acid; nitrogen; marble
   c) global; carbon; energy

2. a) Parts per million

b)

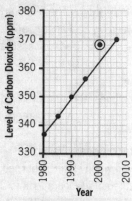

Concentration of CO₂ (ppm) vs Year graph, from 300 to 370 ppm, years 1960 to 2000.

c) It's increasing

d) More fossil fuels are being burned; deforestation.

Page 59 – Skills Practice

1. a) and b)

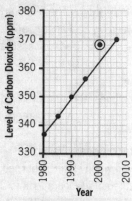

Level of Carbon Dioxide (ppm) vs Year graph, 330 to 380, years 1980 to 2010.

c) The result for the year 2000 should be circled. It could have been misread; there could have been a problem with the equipment used; a lot of carbon dioxide was in the air that particular day.

2. Any answer from 390ppm to 392ppm

3. a) **Any one from:** it would be more reliable; any anomalous results will be easy to spot; the pattern would be easier to see.

b) It would take more time / be more expensive to take more readings.

SPEEDING UP, SLOWING DOWN

Page 63 – Quick Test

1. Distance and time

2. 25m/s

---

3. **Any sensible answers, e.g.:** a ball slows down as friction acts on it; a ball stops as a goalkeeper catches it.

4. **Any sensible answers, e.g.:** a car accelerates as the engine drives it forwards; a planet changes direction as it orbits the Sun.

(Note that the answers to questions 3 and 4 can be the same).

Page 64 – Key Words Exercise

Acceleration – A change in velocity

Balanced – When two forces in opposite directions are equal

Drag force – The force experienced by a moving object in a gas or liquid that opposes its motion

Friction – A force that opposes motion and produces heat energy

Gradient – Equal to velocity on a distance–time graph

Speed – The distance an object moves in a certain time

Stationary – An object that's not moving

Streamlined – An object that's shaped so that the drag force is less

Terminal velocity – The maximum velocity reached by a skydiver when the drag force balances the weight

Unbalanced – When two forces in opposite directions aren't equal

Unit – This must be the same when comparing the speeds of two different objects

Velocity – Speed in a specific direction

Page 64 – Comprehension

1. In the opposite direction to the motion.

2. It increases it.

3. It has a pointed nose and a streamlined torpedo shape.

4. Designers of submarines, boats and cruise liners can improve their designs and make them faster and more efficient.

Page 65 – Testing Understanding

1. a) time; distance
   b) direction; unit; second
   c) Acceleration; force; speed / direction; direction / speed

2. a) The velocity also starts off at almost zero and increases over the first 40s.
   b) They are unbalanced.
   c) i) 50m/s
      ii) It's constant at 50m/s.
   d) They are balanced.

Page 66 – Skills Practice

1. A stopwatch

2. Any sensible answer, e.g.:

Animal	Distance (m)	Time (s)	Time (s) (repeated)	Time (s) (average)	Speed of Plasticine Falling (m/s)
Cheetah					
Dolphin					
Elephant					
Eagle					

3. The idea is to test the streamlining of each shape, so it's fairer to keep the mass the same and change the shape. Otherwise, the test will be investigating a relationship between the size or mass of the animal and its speed.

4. The faster animals have more streamlined shapes.

5. **Any sensible answers, e.g.:** some animals travel in water, others in air, others on land; the animals are different sizes; the animals have different strengths.

SOCIAL INTERACTION

Page 70 – Quick Test

1. Behaviour

2. A stimulus

3. It stays inside its food source, away from predators

4. Courtship

5. Social (behaviour)

Page 71 – Key Words Exercise

Behaviour – The pattern of responses of individuals to a stimulus or stimuli

Courtship display – Behaviour designed to allow reproduction to occur

Fertilisation – The fusing of male and female nuclei

Habit – Learned behaviour gained by a series of steps

Mating – The meeting of a male and female for reproduction

Population – The total number of individuals of the same species in an area

Response – The action made due to receiving a stimulus

Species – Similar organisms able to breed to produce fertile offspring

Status – An individual's position within a group

Stimulus – Something that causes a response in the nervous system

Page 71 – Comprehension

1. The period when male and female deers are found together for mating.

2. a) They are able to see if they are well matched and one can back down without a fight if necessary, so preventing injury.
   b) The strongest stag mates with more deer. The 'best' genes are then passed on to the next generation.

3. To attract females (hinds) and to maintain the group.

4. To feed it with milk and so that it can learn the necessary behaviour for survival.

Page 72 – Testing Understanding

1. a) behaviour; changes
   b) responses; protect / guard
   c) learn / adopt; status; mating
   d) social

2. a)

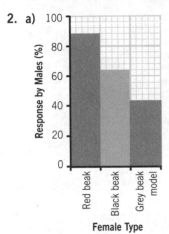

Female Type

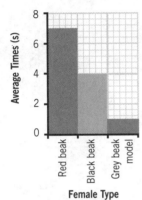

Female Type

   b) The red-beaked female caused more response than the black-beaked female and the males didn't pay much attention to the model.
   c) The length of the courtship behaviour followed the same pattern as the number of responses (i.e. the courtship behaviour of males towards the red-beaked females lasted longer than towards the black-beaked females, and the shortest courtship behaviour was towards the grey-beaked model).
   d) The male finches respond to red-beaked females more than to black beaked and aren't responsive to models or grey-beaked females.
   e) The female finches and the colours of their beaks.

Page 73 – Skills Practice

1.

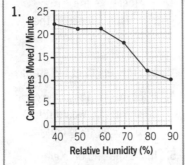

2. Temperature; amount of light; amount of liquid in the dish; the woodlice were of a similar size.

3. Centimetres moved per minute.

4. They should have been kept in identical conditions, preferably at a relative humidity of less than 40%.

5. a) To remove any interaction between individuals in the dish.
   b) To make sure the results were reliable; to make sure the results were all the same pattern; to remove the effect of any 'freak' results ('**to make it a fair test' is not acceptable**).

6. They move less in conditions of higher humidity, which would help them retain water for gas exchange / breathing. In addition, the higher the humidity, the more likely it is that the place would be dark and sheltered, so they would be less likely to be eaten by predators.

USING CHEMISTRY

Page 77 – Quick Test

1. A substance that can be burned to release heat energy.

2. Water (vapour) and carbon dioxide

3. Water (vapour)

4. In factories

5. In a reaction, the total mass of the reactants is equal to the total mass of the products.

6. It combines with oxygen, and oxygen has mass.

Page 78 – Key Words Exercise

Complete combustion – When a material is completely burned in a good supply of oxygen
Displacement reaction – A reaction in which a more reactive metal takes the place of a less reactive metal
Fuel – A substance that can be burned to release heat energy
Hydrocarbon – A compound that contains only carbon and hydrogen
Incomplete combustion – When a material is burned in a limited supply of oxygen
Limewater – A solution of calcium hydroxide that turns cloudy if carbon dioxide gas is bubbled through it
Photosynthesis – The process by which green plants make glucose
Synthetic material – A material that's made in a factory

Page 78 – Comprehension

1. In 1733

2. His mother died when he was seven years old.

3. It's needed for things to burn and for iron to rust.

4. In the manufacture of fizzy drinks.

5. He expressed support for the French Revolution and his home was attacked by an angry mob.

6. He established a church and continued his scientific work to improve people's lives.

Page 79 – Testing Understanding

1. a) fuel; hydrocarbons
   b) incomplete; monoxide
   c) copper; magnesium sulfate; heat / thermal; temperature; energy / heat
   d) made / formed / produced; reactants; products; rearranged

2. a)

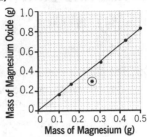

   b) The greater the mass of magnesium burned, the greater the mass of magnesium oxide produced.
   c) The result at 0.26, 0.32 should be circled. The results may have been misread; some of the magnesium oxide may have escaped.

Page 80 – Skills Practice

1. a) Mg
   b) Cu
   c) Fe

2.

Metals Used	Voltage (V)
Iron and copper	0.78
Magnesium and copper	2.71
Iron and magnesium	1.93

3.

Variable Changed	(Combination of) metals used
Variable Measured	Voltage
Variable Kept the Same	Type of fruit

4.

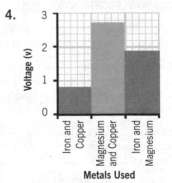

Metals Used

5. a) Magnesium and copper
   b) Iron and copper
   c) The greater the difference in reactivity, the greater the voltage produced; the smaller the difference in reactivity, the lower the voltage produced.

SPACE AND GRAVITY

Page 84 – Quick Test

1. Copernicus

2. The church leaders, because they believed that God had placed the Earth at the centre of the Universe.

3. Their mass and the distance between them.

4. Because the apples only have a small mass.

Page 85 – Key Words Exercise

Big Bang – Scientists' model for the beginning of the Universe
Black hole – The gravity of this is so strong that not even light can escape
Geocentric – A model of the Solar System with the Earth at the centre
Heliocentric – A model of the Solar System with the Sun at the centre
Helium – The product of a nuclear reaction inside a burning star
Hydrogen – The fuel of a star
Nebula – A cloud of gas and dust
Neutron star – The dense core of a star left after a super nova
Red giant – A star that has run out of fuel becomes this
Super nova – A massive star dies in a big explosion known as this
White dwarf – The small, dense core of a dying star

Page 85 – Comprehension

1. He observed nebula in galaxies that were outside the Milky Way.

2. He proved that the Universe was much larger than people believed.

3. The Big Bang theory

4. It can be repaired by astronauts whilst in orbit.

Page 86 – Testing Understanding

1. a) gravity; temperature; nuclear; energy; helium
   b) core; hydrogen; red; white
   c) explode; gravity; light

2. a) It is strongest.
   b) It is weakest.
   c) It is fastest.
   d) It is slowest.

Page 87 – Skills Practice

1. The mass of the Plasticine

2. The force

3. a) She could ask a friend to help her spin the masses at the same speed, for example, once every second. As long as the length of the string is kept constant (and therefore the circumference of the circle), the speed will be constant.
   b) The length of the string

4. If the mass of Plasticine came off the string, would it hit anyone or anything breakable?

5. In a table and on a graph

ACKNOWLEDGEMENTS

The authors and publisher are grateful to the copyright holders for permission to use quoted materials and images.

Every effort has been made to trace copyright holders and obtain their permission for the use of copyright material. The authors and publishers will gladly receive information enabling them to rectify any error or omission in subsequent editions. All facts are correct at time of going to press.

Letts and Lonsdale
4 Grosvenor Place
London SW1X 7DL

Orders: 015395 64910
Enquiries: 015395 65921
Email: enquiries@lettsandlonsdale.co.uk
Website: www.lettsandlonsdale.com

ISBN: 978-1844191-32-1

01/200209

Published by Letts and Lonsdale

© 2009 Letts and Lonsdale.

British Library Cataloguing in Publication Data.

A CIP record of this book is available from the British Library.

Book Concept and Development: Helen Jacobs
Commissioning Editor: Rebecca Skinner
Authors: Emma Poole, Caroline Reynolds and Bob Woodcock
Project Editor: Richard Toms
Cover Design: Angela English
Inside Concept Design: Helen Jacobs and Sarah Duxbury
Text Design and Layout: Paul Oates
Artwork: Letts and Lonsdale

Printed and bound in Italy

Letts and Lonsdale make every effort to ensure that all paper used in our books is made from wood pulp obtained from well-managed forests, controlled sources and recycled wood or fibre.

Skills Practice

Selma and Bezede decide to investigate how the pressure of a gas varies as the gas is heated.

They have some gas sealed in a test tube with a rubber bung.

They use a pressure sensor and a temperature sensor connected to a data logger to measure the pressure in the gas as the temperature rises.

They set up some equipment as shown below.

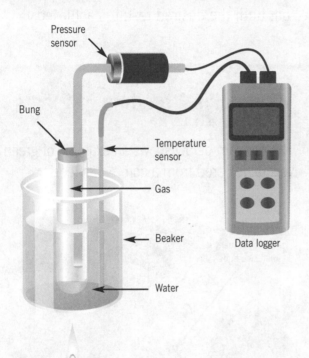

1. Explain why it's better to heat the gas using water in a beaker rather than apply heat directly to the gas using a Bunsen burner.

2. Selma predicts that the temperature of the gas will increase from room temperature to 90°C in about 6 minutes. Selma and Bezede need to program the data logger to take readings at suitable time intervals. Suggest how frequently the data logger should be programmed to take readings.

3. The results of the experiment are recorded in the table below. Carefully choose a suitable scale and plot a graph of pressure (y-axis) against temperature (x-axis) for the gas.

Time (s)	Pressure (N/m^2)	Temperature (°C)
0	101 000	20.0
30	102 300	23.5
60	103 600	27.0
90	104 600	30.5
120	104 900	34.0
150	106 200	37.5
180	107 500	41.0
210	108 800	44.5
240	110 100	48.0
270	111 400	51.5
300	112 700	55.0
330	114 000	58.5
360	115 300	62.0
390	116 600	65.5
420	117 900	69.0
450	119 200	72.5
480	120 500	76.0
510	121 800	79.5
540	123 100	83.0
570	124 400	86.5
600	125 700	90.0

4. Explain, in words, the relationship between the pressure and the temperature of the gas.

Manipulating the Environment

Selective Breeding

Selective breeding is breeding for a desired characteristic. The idea is that new varieties of organisms can be bred by taking advantage of variation:

- Organisms with a desired characteristic are bred with similar organisms.

- This results in offspring, some of which will have an exaggerated version of this characteristic.
- These offspring are then bred again, and so on, until the desired result is achieved.

Selective Breeding in Animals

The diagram below illustrates how new varieties can be produced. Black patches have been selected as the desired characteristic to produce spotty dogs (Dalmatians).

1st generation

2nd generation

3rd generation

In farming, selective breeding is carried out to improve the stock and to develop new varieties of produce. For example, farmers might breed...

- short-legged sheep on upland farms
- cattle that grow to maturity more quickly and produce more beef
- cows that give greater yields of milk
- hens that lay more eggs.

Selective Breeding in Plants

The diagram below shows an example of green vegetables bred from a common ancestor.

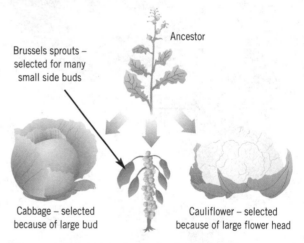

Ancestor

Brussels sprouts – selected for many small side buds

Cabbage – selected because of large bud

Cauliflower – selected because of large flower head

Many well-known fruit and vegetables would be strange-looking things to someone who lived 300 years ago. This is because they've been bred selectively to create products that consumers prefer. However, it takes many generations to get the desired result.

Seedless orange

Wheat with greater seed heads

Dangers of Selective Breeding

Too much selective breeding can cause individual genes to be lost from the breeding population. The loss of a particular characteristic is something to avoid because once it's gone, it's gone forever.

This means there's a loss of variation in the population. Rare breed sanctuaries look after breeds that are no longer used on farms so that useful genes aren't lost forever.

How Human Activities Affect the Environment

Burning fossil fuels, cutting down trees, using pesticides and using fertilisers are examples of how human activity can affect the environment.

Example	Effect on the Environment
Burning fossil fuels and cutting down trees	Fossil fuels (i.e. coal, oil and gas) are being burned at a great rate for electricity and transport. Trees and other plants are also being removed at a great rate for farming or to build homes. These activities contribute to the thickening of the layer of carbon dioxide in the atmosphere and to an increase in the Earth's temperature (global warming). See page 56 for further information.
Pesticides	Pesticides may be washed off the land and into lakes and ponds. Once inside an organism, the pesticide may not break down and may stay in the organism. The food chain below shows how this could affect different organisms: pondweed → tadpole → minnow → perch → heron • A pesticide is taken up by pondweed, which is then eaten by tadpoles. • Each minnow eats a lot of tadpoles, so the amount of pesticide builds up inside it, and each perch eats many minnows. The build-up of chemicals inside an organism is called bioaccumulation. • As a result of bioaccumulation, the levels of pesticide in the herons could be very high. This could weaken the herons' eggshells, making it difficult for the eggs to be incubated without breaking. This might cause a decline in the number of herons.
Fertilisers	If fertilisers run off into water they may cause lots of plants, especially algae, to grow: • At first, this is good because it provides food for animals and supports the food web. • But as the plants die, the microorganisms that decay them use up the oxygen in the water in respiration. This may cause fish to die and could eventually make the entire water stagnant and useless. This process is called eutrophication.

Manipulating the Environment

Energy in Food Chains

Look at the food chain and pyramid of numbers shown opposite:

- The grass uses energy from sunlight to make food by photosynthesis. But most of the light either misses the leaf, is reflected from the leaf or misses the chlorophyll in the leaf, so it isn't used. Actually very little light energy, as a proportion of the total, is used by green plants for photosynthesis.
- The rabbit eats the grass as its energy source. It either uses the energy for respiration, when it's transformed to heat energy and radiated away, or it's not digested and is removed in faeces. In addition, some energy is excreted in urine. So, the rabbit doesn't keep a lot of energy for the fox to use.
- The fox is just like the rabbit in that it loses a lot of energy too. This is why a rabbit has to eat a lot of grass and foxes have to eat a lot of rabbits to obtain enough energy.

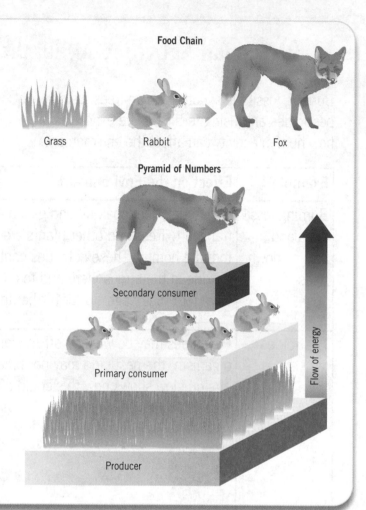

Food Chain

Grass → Rabbit → Fox

Pyramid of Numbers

Secondary consumer

Primary consumer

Producer

Flow of energy

Effects on the Energy in Food Chains

It's very important to check any potential environmental effects before introducing any changes to a food chain. If people are going to manipulate the environment to their needs, they must be sure of the consequences. Here are two examples:

- **Limiting factors** that reduce the rate of photosynthesis (e.g. the availability of water, light and carbon dioxide, or the amount of chlorophyll) will reduce the amount of energy available in a food chain.
- Changing genes that alter plants to make them outcompete others may affect the energy flow through a system.

Changing Genes – Good or Bad?

Genetic modification…
- is sometimes referred to as genetic engineering
- involves changing genes in organisms, sometimes between different organisms.

For example, a gene from a fish that produces a kind of antifreeze could be added to a tomato to enable it to grow at lower temperatures. The tomato would then be called a **GMO** (genetically modified organism).

This kind of tomato would cost less to grow and could be grown over a longer period. As a result, the grower could make more profit and it would cost the customer less. But is this a good thing?

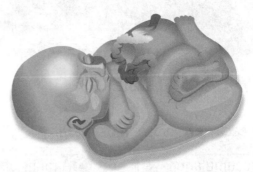

Stem cells…
- come from either **embryonic** cells (originating from fertilised human eggs) or from the umbilical cords of newborn babies
- can grow into any type of cell.

Consider that stem cells could be grown into brain cells to help sufferers of Parkinson's disease. The cells could be implanted into the patient's brain to replace cells damaged by the disease. Do you think this is a good idea?

A number of questions have to be addressed to reach an answer that meets human needs without damaging the environment (i.e. **sustainable development**):
- Is it right to genetically modify human cells to try to cure cancers or diseases like cystic fibrosis?
- Should the research into these new technologies be carried out on humans or animals? Would you volunteer to take part in tests?
- What effect might genetic modification have on the environment?

Quick Test

1. What is selective breeding?
2. What is the main danger of selective breeding?
3. What is the main gas contributing to global warming?
4. What gas do the microorganisms of decay use up?
5. Why are food chains usually very short (only three to five steps)?
6. What is a GMO?

KEY WORDS
Make sure you understand these words before moving on!
- Bioaccumulation
- Embryonic
- Eutrophication
- Global warming
- GMO
- Limiting factors
- Selective breeding
- Stem cell
- Sustainable development
- Varieties

Manipulating the Environment

Key Words Exercise

Match each key word with its meaning.

Key word	Meaning
Bioaccumulation	A range of different types within the same species
Embryonic	A cell able to develop into many different types
Eutrophication	Using variation to breed a desired characteristic into the offspring
Global warming	An increase in the Earth's temperature caused by the thickening of the layer of carbon dioxide in the atmosphere
GMO	An increase in the concentration of something along a food chain
Limiting factors	Caused by fertilisers in water, leading to stagnation
Selective breeding	Environmental changes that alter a reaction like photosynthesis
Stem cell	An organism that has had its genetic make-up artificially altered
Sustainable development	Meeting human needs without damaging the environment
Varieties	Originating from the developing fertilised egg

Comprehension

Read the passage about organic farming, then answer the following questions.

1 What does the term 'biodegradable' mean?

2 Why is it important that the compost heap is turned over to allow oxygen into it?

3 How does digging compost back into the soil add nutrients?

4 Light and water are two environmental factors needed for photosynthesis. Why might these be limiting factors if the plants were grown in the wrong places?

5 How might the appearance of cabbages grown organically differ from those grown using pesticides and herbicides?

In organic farming, all biodegradable waste material is composted and dug back into the soil. This means placing all grass clippings, vegetable peelings, old leaves and dead plants in a large heap. This pile is turned over occasionally to make sure oxygen gets to all parts of it. After several months, you have excellent compost that adds nutrients to the soil as well as improving the soil structure.

Plants are only grown where the conditions suit them. If the plant likes shade, then it's not grown in full sunlight. If the plant likes to be well-drained, it's not grown in heavy clay, which doesn't drain away water easily.

No artificial fertilisers, herbicides or pesticides are used. Often slugs, snails and caterpillars are picked off by hand. Netting is used as a physical barrier to flying pests. Weed growth is restricted by growing through plastic sheeting or by mulching the soil with materials like bark chippings.

Testing Understanding

1 **Fill in the missing words to complete the sentences about the effects of pesticides on food webs.**

a) Chemicals are often used to increase crop _____, improve appearance and remove competition. But they also have negative effects on food webs and wildlife.

b) Pesticides, a general name for fungicides, insecticides and rodenticides, are, as their name suggests, used to combat the problem of _____. They have improved the appearance of our fruit and _____, which are no longer ravaged by pests such as caterpillars, _____ (aphids) or field mice.

c) However, killing populations of pests drastically affects _____ webs. For example, imagine that thrushes eat insects and slugs; if all the _____ were killed by insecticides, the thrushes' _____ source would be severely _____ and thus the numbers of thrushes would also be reduced. The consequence of this is that _____ would have _____ predators and may, therefore, flourish. They will in turn eat _____ of the food crop.

d) _____ can also be washed into ponds and lakes, where they are broken up by microscopic plants. At this stage they're very _____, but become more and more _____ at every stage of the food chain. Eventually they become concentrated enough to _____. This is called _____.

2 **Read the information about the effect of DDT on peregrines, then answer the questions that follow.**

Extensive use of the insecticide DDT, to kill insects, during the 1950s resulted in a marked decline in the number of peregrine falcons. DDT can't be excreted by animals that eat it and the accumulation of the poison in the falcons caused them to produce very thin eggshells that often cracked, killing the chick.

The following data refers to the number of sightings of peregrines after the use of such pesticides was banned:

Year	1964	1966	1968	1970	1972	1974	1976	1978	1980	1982	1984	1986
No. of Sightings	4	5	4	6	7	6	12	11	15	22	43	76

a) Plot this data in the form of a bar graph.
b) Suggest how many sightings there may have been in 1985.
c) In which year would the number of sightings have been approximately 33?
d) How many years did it take for the peregrine population to treble?
e) Peregrines eat mainly small mammals, so why did an insecticide nearly wipe them out?

Manipulating the Environment

Hardeep and Sue were doing an experiment in plots in the school garden. They planted carrots into six different plots.

At the start of the experiment, immediately before planting, they added an artificial fertiliser, Vegegrow, to the plots in different amounts.

Each plot was treated in the same way every day. After several months, they carefully dug up the carrots, and washed and dried them before weighing them.

Their results are shown in the table below.

Plot	1	2	3	4	5	6
Amount of Fertiliser (g)	0	4	8	12	16	20
Average Mass of Carrot (g)	262	322	368	402	404	398

1. Draw a bar graph to show how the average mass of carrot varied from plot to plot.

2. Why didn't adding more fertiliser make much difference in plots 5 and 6?

3. What are the environmental dangers of adding too much fertiliser?

4. What is the dependent variable in this investigation?

5. What variables would need to be controlled in order to make this a fair test?

Environmental Chemistry

The Changing Environment

The environment is changed by...
- human activities
- natural processes.

Scientists around the world work together to monitor these changes and to develop ideas that have changed the way that people think and behave.

What is in Soil?

Soils contain...
- **weathered** pieces of rock of different shapes and sizes
- different amounts of water
- bacteria and **fungi**, which decompose organic material and release minerals that can be used by new plants
- animals, such as earthworms and moles. Earthworms improve the soil by aerating it and by dragging organic material, such as leaves, down from the surface of the soil.

Soils also contain a dark, sticky material called **humus**. Humus...
- is the remains of dead plants and animals that have rotted away
- contains minerals that help new plants to grow
- helps to stick the rock particles together and helps to hold water.

Plants grow best in soils that have high levels of humus.

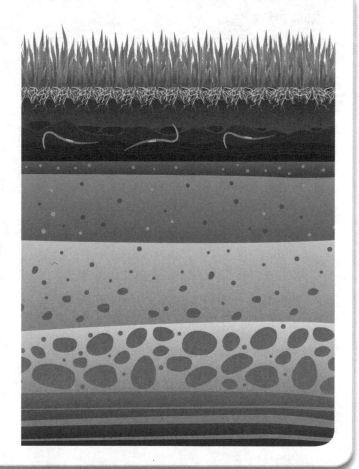

Satellites

Satellites can be used to take photographs of the Earth's surface. Some plants grow particularly well in certain types of soil.

Scientists can use these satellite photographs to...
- monitor which plants are growing
- identify the type of soil and the underlying rock.

Environmental Chemistry

The pH of Soils

Most soils have a **pH** range of 4 to 8. Soils...
- in limestone areas typically have a pH of about 8
- that have high levels of humus or are in areas affected by **acid rain** tend to be slightly acidic.

Most crops only grow well in soils that have a certain pH range.

Plant	Preferred pH Range
Potato	4.5–6.0
Carrot	5.5–7.0
Pea	6.0–7.5

If a soil becomes too...
- acidic, farmers can add powdered lime (calcium carbonate) or **quicklime** (calcium hydroxide)
- alkaline, farmers can add manure. As the manure rots down, it produces acids that reduce the pH of the soil.

Weathering

Over time, rocks are broken into smaller pieces.

Chalk, limestone and marble all contain the chemical compound calcium carbonate ($CaCO_3$). These rocks, and building materials made from these rocks, are chemically weathered.

In areas of high rainfall and where air pollution has produced acid rain, the rocks are weathered more quickly.

Acid Rain

The atmosphere contains a small amount of carbon dioxide. It's produced...
- when animals and plants respire
- by volcanic activity
- by the burning of **fossil fuels**, such as coal, oil and natural gas, which contain carbon.

Carbon dioxide dissolves in moisture to produce weakly acidic rainwater. Normal rainwater has a pH of about 5.6.

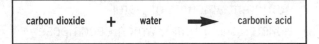

carbon dioxide + water → carbonic acid

Sulfur dioxide and nitrogen oxides lower the pH of rainwater even more to form acid rain, which typically has a pH of 3 to 5.

Sulfur dioxide is a toxic and corrosive gas that's produced by...
- volcanic activity
- the burning of fossil fuels, many of which contain traces of sulfur.

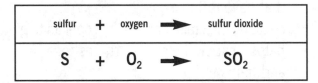

sulfur + oxygen → sulfur dioxide

$$S + O_2 \rightarrow SO_2$$

The sulfur dioxide dissolves in rainwater to form acid rain or, if it's very cold, acid snow. Acid rain affects wildlife, rocks and metals.

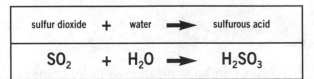

sulfur dioxide + water → sulfurous acid

$$SO_2 + H_2O \rightarrow H_2SO_3$$

Nitrogen oxides (NO_x) are produced by...
- lightning strikes
- the burning of fossil fuels
- the high temperatures produced by car exhausts.

The Effects of Acid Rain

Acid rain can...
- kill trees
- kill plants and animals living in affected lakes
- dissolve rocks that contain metal carbonates (for example, limestone, marble and chalk, which contain calcium carbonate)
- damage statues and buildings made from rocks that contain metal carbonates
- corrode metals such as iron.

In lakes, the eggs of fish can also be damaged as the acidity increases. Young fish can be born deformed or may not hatch at all, while other organisms may grow more quickly.

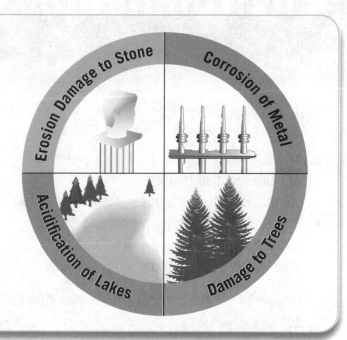

Reducing the Effects of Acid Rain

Neutralisation reactions can reduce the effects of acid rain:
- Powdered lime can be added to affected lakes. Lime neutralises the acidic compounds in the water.
- Acidic soils can be neutralised by adding powdered limestone (calcium carbonate) or quicklime (calcium hydroxide), which neutralise the acidic compounds in the soil.

When fossil fuels are burned, the amount of sulfur dioxide released into the atmosphere can be reduced by...
- removing sulfur from oil and natural gas before they're burned
- installing 'scrubbers' in power stations to remove sulfur dioxide from the exhaust gases produced when coal is burned
- using low-sulfur coals.

Atmospheric Pollution

Carbon dioxide is produced when all living things respire, and it's taken in when plants photosynthesise. But this balance has been upset by human activities, such as...
- people burning more fossil fuels
- forests being cut down for timber, for mining and to build new roads or homes.

Deforestation means that there are fewer trees left to photosynthesise, so less carbon dioxide is removed from the atmosphere. Some people remove trees by burning them, which increases the carbon dioxide in the atmosphere.

Scientists monitor the levels of pollutant gases in the atmosphere. The amount of carbon dioxide is so low that it's measured in 'parts per million' (ppm), but the increase of this gas in the atmosphere is a concern.

Scientists are particularly concerned about the loss of trees in tropical rainforests. They believe that some species may become extinct and there will be less variation in the species that survive.

Environmental Chemistry

Global Warming

Scientists believe that the Earth is warming up. Their evidence includes...
- an increase in the average global temperature
- some areas becoming wetter and others becoming drier, leading to enormous disruption to agriculture
- a decrease in the amount of Arctic sea ice
- a rise in sea levels as ice melts and seawater expands as it's warmed
- an increase in extreme weather events around the world (e.g. flooding and hurricanes).

The Greenhouse Effect

The **greenhouse effect** is causing global warming. A greenhouse effect occurs naturally on Earth. Without it, the Earth would be much cooler and life may not have developed:
- A layer of carbon dioxide and other greenhouse gases, such as methane, act as a blanket around the Earth.
- Radiation from the Sun warms the surface of the Earth. As the heat energy is reflected into space, some is trapped by the carbon dioxide in the atmosphere, so the Earth warms up.
- The more carbon dioxide in the atmosphere, the more heat energy is trapped and the warmer the Earth becomes.

Scientists believe that human activities, such as the burning of fossil fuels, are increasing the warming of the Earth at a dramatic rate.

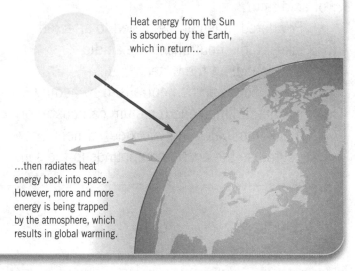

Heat energy from the Sun is absorbed by the Earth, which in return...

...then radiates heat energy back into space. However, more and more energy is being trapped by the atmosphere, which results in global warming.

Quick Test

1. Humus is found in soil. What is humus?
2. Suggest how a farmer could reduce the pH level of an alkaline soil.
3. Why is rainwater naturally acidic?
4. How is acid rain formed?
5. How are nitrogen oxides produced naturally?
6. Name two greenhouse gases.

KEY WORDS
Make sure you understand these words before moving on!
- Acid rain
- Carbonic acid
- Deforestation
- Fossil fuels
- Fungi
- Greenhouse effect
- Humus
- Neutralisation
- pH
- Quicklime
- Satellite
- Sulfur dioxide
- Weathered

Key Words Exercise

Match each key word with its meaning.

Acid rain • • A chemical, formed when carbon dioxide dissolves in water, which makes normal rainwater slightly acidic

Carbonic acid • • Calcium hydroxide

Deforestation • • The cutting down of large numbers of trees

Fossil fuels • • The reaction between an acid and an alkali

Fungi • • How gases, including carbon dioxide and methane, cause the Earth to warm up

Greenhouse effect • • A toxic gas formed when sulfur is burned

Humus • • A type of microbe that decomposes plant and animal material

Neutralisation • • A scale used to measure how acidic or alkaline something is

pH • • When a rock is broken down into smaller pieces

Quicklime • • An object that orbits a larger body

Satellite • • A type of rain formed in polluted areas when sulfur oxides or nitrogen oxides dissolve in water

Sulfur dioxide • • Non-renewable energy resources, such as coal, oil and natural gas, formed from plants and animals that lived long ago

Weathered • • Dark, sticky material formed when plant and animal matter rots

Comprehension

Read the passage about lichens, then answer the following questions.

1 Name two types of animal that live in lichens.

2 Why are lichens useful to people?

3 What is a symbiotic relationship?

4 What benefits does each plant bring to their relationship?

5 If the number of types of lichen growing in a city decreases, what does this indicate?

Lichens are commonly found on trees, rocks and walls. They come in a wide range of colours and sizes, and provide homes for spiders and insects. People use them in the manufacture of some sunscreens and antibiotics.

Lichens aren't single plants. Each lichen is made up of two plants that live together. The plants have a symbiotic relationship; each plant benefits from the presence of the other. One plant is a fungus and the other is a green alga. The alga can photosynthesise to provide food for both plants, while the fungus creates a 'thallus' that houses both plants.

Lichens are very useful as environmental or bio indicators. They're very sensitive to air pollution. Generally, the smaller the number of species of lichen growing in an area, the more polluted the air is. Lichens are very sensitive to sulfur dioxide pollution in the air. Since the levels of sulfur dioxide pollution have fallen over the last 30 years, the number of species of lichen growing in urban areas has greatly increased.

Environmental Chemistry

Testing Understanding

1 **Fill in the missing words to complete the sentences about environmental chemistry.**

a) Most soils have a _____ between 4 and 8. Soils in limestone areas are slightly _____ and have a pH of around 8, while soils in polluted areas may be slightly _____ and have a lower pH. If a soil is too acidic, farmers can add calcium carbonate (lime) or calcium hydroxide (_____) to increase its pH. If a soil is too _____, farmers can add manure to the soil. As the manure rots, it produces acidic compounds that _____ the pH of the soil.

b) Normal rainwater is slightly acidic because the gas, _____ dioxide, dissolves in the water to form carbonic acid. In polluted areas, sulfur dioxide may also dissolve in the rainwater to form _____ rain. Acid rain can also be produced by _____ oxides. Acid rain can damage buildings made from rocks that contain the chemical compound calcium carbonate, such as limestone, chalk or _____ .

c) The greenhouse effect is causing _____ warming. A layer of greenhouse gases, including _____ dioxide and methane, acts as a blanket around the Earth. This layer stops some heat _____ from escaping into space, so the planet warms up.

2 **Read the information about carbon dioxide in the atmosphere, then answer the questions that follow.**

The amount of carbon dioxide in the atmosphere is changing. The table below shows the amount of carbon dioxide gas in the atmosphere at different times.

a) What does 'ppm' mean?
b) Copy the axes opposite and plot the results as a line graph.
c) What is happening to the level of carbon dioxide in the atmosphere?
d) Suggest why the level of carbon dioxide in the atmosphere is changing.

Year	Concentration of Carbon Dioxide (ppm)
1960	315
1970	328
1980	342
1990	356
2000	369

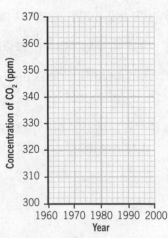

Skills Practice

A scientist wanted to know if the level of carbon dioxide in the air had changed over time.

Every five years, she returned to the same road and measured the level of carbon dioxide in the air. The table below shows her results.

Year	Level of Carbon Dioxide (ppm)
1980	336
1985	344
1990	350
1995	357
2000	368
2005	370

1 a) Use the results in the table to draw a line graph. Remember to label both axes and plot the results carefully.

   b) Add a line of best fit.

   c) Circle the anomalous result and suggest why this result might be anomalous.

2 Predict what the level of carbon dioxide will be in 2020.

3 A second scientist suggests monitoring the levels of carbon dioxide in the road every six months.

   a) Give a possible advantage of the second scientist's method.

   b) Give a possible disadvantage of the second scientist's method.

Speeding Up, Slowing Down

Speed

When you want to describe how fast something is moving, you measure its **speed**. Speed is a measure of how far an object travels in a specific time.

To determine the speed of an object, you need two pieces of information:

- The distance it has travelled.
- The time it has taken.

Speed is calculated using this equation:

$$\text{speed} = \frac{\text{distance}}{\text{time}}$$

The cyclist below travels between the two lamp posts in 5.0 seconds. The distance between the lamp posts is 100 metres.

The speed is equal to $\dfrac{100m}{5.0s} = 20m/s$.

This calculation gives the average speed of the cyclist since his actual speed may vary over the 5.0 seconds.

Some measuring instruments are designed for specific jobs and can give a direct measurement of speed:

- A policeman uses a radar gun to obtain measurements of distance and time. The radar gun then calculates the speed.
- An anemometer is a device designed specifically to measure the speed of the wind.

Units

Metres per second (m/s) is a commonly used **unit** for speed, but sometimes different units are used:

- Road signs in Britain use the unit miles per hour (mph) but most other European countries use kilometres per hour (km/h).

- It would be easier to measure the speed of a snail in a smaller unit, such as centimetres per second (cm/s).

All of the units for speed are a distance unit divided by a time unit. If you want to compare the speeds of two different objects, you must use the same unit of speed for both objects.

Velocity

Velocity is a speed in a particular direction. The two cars below have the same speed, but different velocities.

20m/s to the left

20m/s to the right

Force and Velocity

A force can change the velocity of an object by...
- making an object go faster
- making an object go slower
- making a **stationary** object move
- making a moving object stop
- changing the direction of a moving object.

The **acceleration** of an object is defined as when the velocity changes. All of the objects below experience acceleration:
- A car speeds up as the engine drives it forwards.
- A ball stops as the goalkeeper catches it.
- A ball slows down as the force of **friction** acts on it.
- The Earth changes direction as it rotates in a circular orbit around the Sun.

On Earth, the force of gravity and usually the force of friction are acting on objects. If there were no forces acting on an object...
- a stationary object would remain stationary
- a moving object would continue to move at the same velocity (i.e. at the same speed in the same direction).

An ice skater experiences very little friction. This is as close as you can get on Earth to an object not having any forces acting on it. The ice skater glides a long way at the same velocity before she finally comes to rest.

Speeding Up, Slowing Down

Friction and Streamlining

Without friction...
- you wouldn't be able to walk
- wheels wouldn't grip on the road.

Brakes rely on friction to slow things down, producing heat energy. Moving parts in engines are oiled to reduce friction so that moving parts don't overheat. Skiers wax their skis to reduce friction, enabling them to go faster.

As objects travel through gases or liquids, frictional forces slow them down:
- These frictional forces are also known as **drag forces**.
- The effect of these forces can be reduced if an object is **streamlined**. A dolphin experiences a small drag force because its shape is very streamlined.

Balanced and Unbalanced Forces

A car engine needs to supply a driving force greater than the drag force, otherwise the car will slow down:

- When the driving force is greater than the drag force, the forces are **unbalanced** and the car accelerates.

- When the drag force is greater than the driving force, the forces are unbalanced and the car slows down.

- When the driving force and the drag force are equal, the forces are **balanced** and the car continues to move at a constant velocity.

A skydiver accelerates under the force of gravity (weight). This force is a downward force:
- As the skydiver falls faster, the upward drag force increases.
- Eventually, the drag force is great enough to balance his weight and the forces are balanced.
- He then falls at a constant speed called **terminal velocity**.

Air resistance

Weight

❶ His weight is greater than the drag force, so he accelerates. He has not yet reached maximum speed.

Air resistance

Weight

❷ His weight is equal to the drag force, so the forces are balanced. He has now reached maximum speed and his velocity is constant.

Describing Motion With Graphs

A distance–time graph illustrates the motion of an object. The **gradient** of the graph is equal to distance divided by time, which is equal to the velocity.

$$\text{gradient} = \text{velocity} = \frac{\text{distance travelled}}{\text{time}}$$

Example	Distance–time Graph
The car is stationary, 40.0m away from a tree.  Distance = 40.0m	The gradient of the line is zero because the velocity of the car is zero. 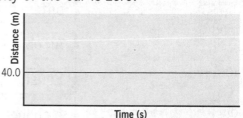
The car is travelling away from the tree. It takes 4.0s to travel 40.0m.  Time in seconds	The distance–time graph has a gradient of 10.0 meaning that the velocity of the car is 10.0m/s. 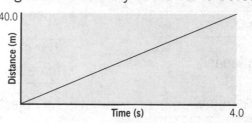
A cyclist travels at a constant speed from point A to B. She stops between B and C, then continues at a constant speed to D. The cyclist stops again between points D and E. Between E and F, the cyclist travels at a slower constant speed in the opposite direction, ending up at the starting position when she reaches point F.	The gradient changes as the velocity changes. 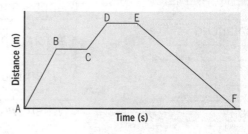

Quick Test

1. What two pieces of information are needed to calculate speed?
2. Calculate the speed of a car that moves 150 metres in 6.0 seconds.
3. Give two examples of a force changing the velocity of an object.
4. Give two examples of an object accelerating.

Speeding Up, Slowing Down

Key Words Exercise

Match each key word with its meaning.

Key word	Meaning
Acceleration	This must be the same when comparing the speeds of two different objects
Balanced	An object that's shaped so that the drag force is less
Drag force	Equal to velocity on a distance–time graph
Friction	A change in velocity
Gradient	The distance an object moves in a certain time
Speed	Speed in a specific direction
Stationary	The maximum velocity reached by a skydiver when the drag force balances the weight
Streamlined	An object that's not moving
Terminal velocity	The force experienced by a moving object in a gas or liquid that opposes its motion
Unbalanced	A force that opposes motion and produces heat energy
Unit	When two forces in opposite directions are equal
Velocity	When two forces in opposite directions aren't equal

Comprehension

Read the passage about drag forces, then answer the following questions.

1 In which direction does a drag force act?

2 What effect does a greater speed have on the drag force?

3 How does a dolphin's body allow it to travel faster?

4 What can be learned from the study of creatures such as dolphins and sharks?

Whenever an object moves through water, it experiences a force called drag, opposing its motion. A stronger drag force means that a greater driving force is required in order to make the object accelerate. Drag forces increase if an object travels at a greater speed.

Dolphins and sharks have pointed noses and torpedo-shaped bodies that are larger at the front than they are at the back. The streamlined shape of their bodies allows them to travel faster though water because the drag force is reduced.

Researchers study the shape of naturally-streamlined creatures. Their research allows them to design boats, cruise liners and submarines that can travel faster and more efficiently.

Testing Understanding

1 **Fill in the missing words to complete the sentences about speeding up and slowing down.**

a) Speed is a measure of how far an object travels in a specific _____. To

determine the speed of an object, you need to know the _____ it has

travelled and the time that it took.

b) Velocity is speed in a specific _____. Both speed and velocity can be measured

in the _____ metres per _____ (m/s).

c) _____ means a change in velocity. A _____ is required

to change a velocity. It can change the velocity of an object by changing its

_____ or by changing its _____.

2 **Study the information about a skydiver, then answer the questions that follow.**

The graph below shows the motion of a skydiver as she jumps out of a hot-air balloon for the first 80 seconds. She doesn't open her parachute during this time.

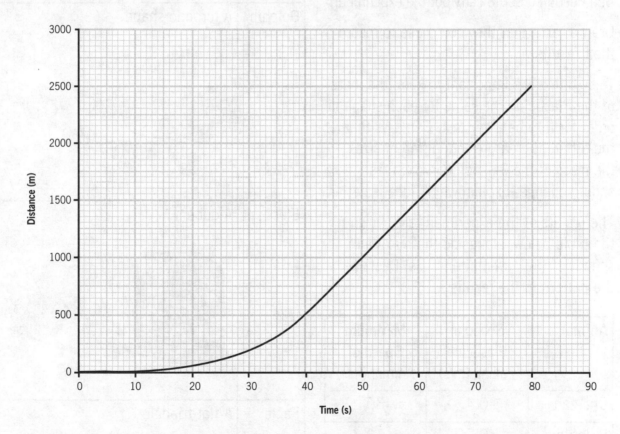

a) The gradient of this distance–time graph starts off at almost zero and then increases over the first 40 seconds of motion. What does this tell you about the velocity of the skydiver over this time?

b) During the period 0–40 seconds, what can you say about the forces on the skydiver?

c) i) Calculate the gradient of the graph between 40s and 80s.

ii) What does this tell you about the velocity of the skydiver between 40s and 80s?

d) What can you say about the forces on the skydiver between 40s and 80s?

Speeding Up, Slowing Down

Tulsy and Ben want to investigate whether there's a relationship between the speed of an animal and its shape.

They have made some shapes from Plasticine and will test how streamlined they are when falling through wallpaper paste.

The shapes they will use to represent each animal are shown in the table opposite.

1. What other piece of equipment do Tulsy and Ben need in order to carry out the experiment?

2. Draw a table that they could use to record their results.

3. Tulsy thinks it's important to keep the mass of the Plasticine the same for each shape in order for it to be a fair test. Ben says that as the different creatures are different sizes, the mass of the Plasticine in each test should change. Explain which idea is better.

4. The results of the experiment are shown in the table below, alongside the maximum speeds of the different animals. Describe the pattern in the results.

Animal	Speed of Plasticine Falling (m/s)	Maximum Speed of Animal (m/s)
Cheetah	0.4	30
Dolphin	0.2	16
Elephant	0.1	10
Eagle	0.3	20

5. Suggest three ways in which this experimental method doesn't model the real-life situation.

Animal	Shape to Represent the Animal
Cheetah	A triangle with a narrow front
Dolphin	A torpedo shape
Elephant	A cube
Eagle	A flat triangle

Social Interaction

Behaviour is the organism's response to changes in its internal or external environment. So, if you wish to observe **responses**, you can investigate them by manipulating the environment and recording the responses.

The table below shows some examples.

Observation Test	Description
Watching woodlice	If a number of woodlice are placed in the centre of a large Petri dish, they will run around very fast in all directions. When they reach the edge of the dish they will slow down and move around the edge, often stopping when they meet another woodlouse. This behaviour can be watched and recorded on film, or the positions of the woodlice plotted every minute or so for a period of time.
Watching maggots	If a narrow beam of light is shone onto a fly maggot's head, it will move away from it. So, you can shine a light on the maggot from one direction and record the response, then repeat it from another direction and so on. If the maggot is covered with a dilute, coloured liquid (that doesn't affect it!), then the trail it leaves behind can be analysed in relation to the light directions.
Watching humans	Humans respond to exercise with increases in heart rate, breathing rate and skin temperature. These responses can be measured before and after vigorous exercise and recorded.

Social Interaction

Benefits of Behaviour

In each example on the previous page, the organisms benefit from the behaviour they show:

- Woodlice – the random running around enables them to find shelter from predators as quickly as possible. Being in touch with an object keeps them protected.
- Maggots – turning away from light keeps them inside the food material (for example, rotting meat) and away from predators.
- Humans – increased breathing and heart rates provide more oxygen to the body and move the blood faster, which means energy gets to the muscles more quickly. The skin temperature rises to cool the blood so that the internal body temperature doesn't rise too high.

Here are some other examples of beneficial behaviour:

- A baby will cry when its nappy is wet to draw attention to itself, so that it can be changed. This prevents the baby becoming uncomfortable and reduces the chances of nappy rash.
- Baby birds will call their parents for food to allow them to grow and develop.
- Parent animals will make warning noises to their young to tell them that they're in danger, as a predator may be around.

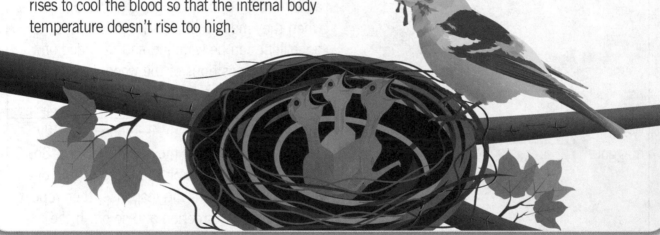

How Plants Behave

Plants don't really show behaviour as such, but they do respond to **stimuli**:

- When a seed germinates (starts to grow), the root always grows down and the shoot always grows up as a response to gravity.
- Young seedlings will grow towards the light when placed on a windowsill.

This behaviour ensures that the leaves are in the best possible light and the roots are in the soil to obtain nutrients.

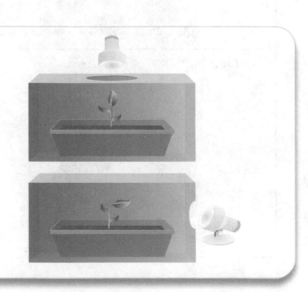

Learning Behaviour

Behaviour is often learned from interaction with other individuals, for example, parents, brothers and sisters, and peers:

- Animals may learn from their parents which foods are good to eat and may learn how to hunt. Play also helps young animals to practise the skills required to survive.
- Within any social group, behaviour is learned to retain the position within it. Gorillas will groom each other to maintain their group position. Male animals will learn how to show that another is superior and therefore will not come to harm.
- **Courtship displays**, including song, often 'mark' territory for a male as well as attract females to it. These behaviours are often learned through experience.
- People learn traditional customs that last for many years to help maintain the community and social life in which they live. You also develop **habits**, which are often very hard to break, through a series of short, learned steps.

In all cases, those organisms that show the most suitable behaviour are the most likely to succeed in terms of producing offspring. This is of huge benefit to the **species** (similar organisms that can **mate** to produce fertile offspring).

Living Together

All animal **populations** (groups of the same species) rely on the behaviour of the individuals in it to survive.

Even solitary animals have to use behavioural responses when they meet another member of the species, or when they need to mate.

Behaviour for Mating

Here are some examples of how different organisms behave at mating time:

- Corals use a variety of environmental signals (e.g. temperature and the cycle of the Moon) to synchronise the release of sperm and eggs into the water. By releasing these at the same time, the corals ensure that the eggs have the best chance of **fertilisation**.
- Male crickets sing when they're ready to mate. The 'song' changes when a female approaches. They touch antennae and mating occurs. The singing increases the chances of males and females meeting, which makes fertilisation more likely.
- Mute swans mate for life, which helps to ensure that eggs are fertilised each year. To maintain the relationship, the pair show courtship display behaviour at mating time.

Social Interaction

Behaviour for Status

Here are some examples of how different social behaviours help individuals and populations to exist side by side in relative comfort and allow successful reproduction:

- When you meet royalty you bow, at least your head, as a means of showing that they have higher status in the population.
- When people meet each other, they often greet each other or shake hands to acknowledge that they don't threaten each other.

- When an inferior lion meets a bigger, stronger lion, it will show respect by backing away and placing its tail between its legs. This prevents fighting and injury to either lion.

This kind of social behaviour is necessary for different species to survive.

Quick Test

1. What is the total response of an organism to changes in the environment called?
2. What is the name given to the factor that's sensed by an organism?
3. What is the benefit to a maggot of turning away from light?
4. What type of behaviour is the display of a male to a female?
5. What is the name given to the interaction behaviour between all members of a group?

KEY WORDS

Make sure you understand these words before moving on!

- Behaviour
- Courtship display
- Fertilisation
- Habit
- Mating
- Population
- Response
- Species
- Status
- Stimulus

Key Words Exercise

Match each key word with its meaning.

Key Word	Meaning
Behaviour	Something that causes a response in the nervous system
Courtship display	The action made due to receiving a stimulus
Fertilisation	The pattern of responses of individuals to a stimulus or stimuli
Habit	The meeting of a male and female for reproduction
Mating	Learned behaviour gained by a series of steps
Population	Behaviour designed to allow reproduction to occur
Response	The total number of individuals of the same species in an area
Species	An individual's position within a group
Status	Similar organisms able to breed to produce fertile offspring
Stimulus	The fusing of male and female nuclei

Comprehension

Read the passage about adult red deer, then answer the following questions.

1. What is meant by the 'rut'?

2. **a)** What is the purpose of the rival stags walking alongside each other?

   b) What is the advantage of this walk and possible fighting?

3. What is the purpose of 'roaring'?

4. Why do you think the hind keeps her offspring with her for one year?

Adult red deer are found in single-sex groups for most of the year. During the mating season, from late August to early winter, called the rut, mature male stags compete for the female hinds. They will challenge each other by walking alongside each other and assessing each other's size, antlers and likely fighting ability. If neither backs down, fighting may break out in which the stags use their antlers to force the other to retreat.

The stronger stags will attract groups of hinds by continuous 'roaring' and this also keeps his harem (the hinds) near to him. The stag will mate with each female in the harem. Each female produces one calf (very occasionally two) after about 8–9 months and keeps it with her for a further year.

Social Interaction

1. **Fill in the missing words to complete the sentences about social interaction.**

   a) The total responses of an individual to its environment are called its _____.
   This allows the individual to adapt to any _____ in the internal or
   external environment.

   b) You can observe _____ by artificially changing the environment. The purpose of
   this behaviour is to survive. It is often to _____ against predators or to
   keep the individual in the most favourable environment.

   c) The parent animal, or interaction with other individuals, helps the young to
   _____ the appropriate behaviour. This helps the youngster to keep its
   place, or _____ in the group, and also allows it to learn how to attract a
   member of the opposite sex for _____.

   d) The overall _____ behaviour has a beneficial effect on the survival of
   the species.

2. **Read the information below, then answer the questions that follow.**

   Male zebra finches show courtship behaviour towards females. An experiment was carried out
   in which male finches were caged with...
   - a female with a red beak (cage A)
   - a female with a black beak (cage B)
   - a model female with a grey beak (cage C).

   These were the results:
   - In cage A, 88% of males showed courtship behaviour for an average of 7 seconds.
   - In cage B, 64% of males showed courtship behaviour for an average of 4 seconds.
   - In cage C, 42% of males showed courtship behaviour for an average of 1 second.

   a) Plot this data in the form of two separate bar graphs, with the females shown on the x-axis.
   b) What conclusion can you make about the number of responses by the males?
   c) What conclusion can you make about the length of the courtship behaviour shown by the males?
   d) What overall conclusion can you make from this data?
   e) What was the independent variable in this experiment?

Shannon and Jason carried out an investigation into the behaviour of woodlice in different humidity levels (the amount of water vapour in the air).

Woodlice are crustaceans, like crabs and shrimps, and breathe through gills, not lungs.

Shannon and Jason set up six Petri dishes, each containing a different and known percentage relative humidity.

A single woodlouse was placed into each dish and the distance it moved in a set period of time was recorded.

This was repeated several times and the average results are given in the table below.

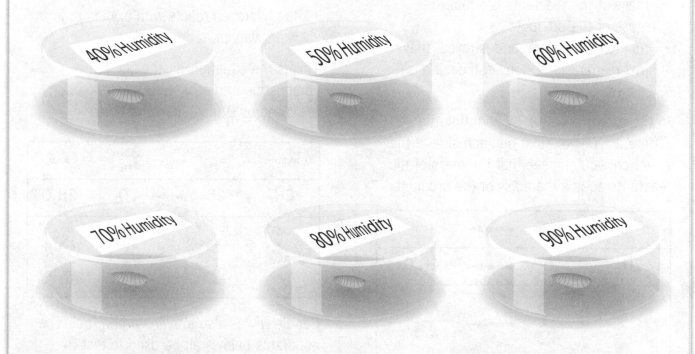

Relative Humidity (%)	40	50	60	70	80	90
Centimetres Moved per Minute	22	21	21	18	12	10

1. Plot the data in the form of a line graph (label the axes clearly).

2. What variables would Shannon and Jason have to assume would remain the same in order to make this investigation a fair test?

3. What is the dependent variable in this investigation?

4. What conditions should the woodlice have been kept in before the experiment?

5. a) Why should only one woodlouse at a time be placed in the Petri dish?
   b) Why did Shannon and Jason repeat this several times?

6. How would the response of woodlice to humidity help them to survive in natural conditions?

Using Chemistry

Conservation of Mass

The chemicals...
- that start a reaction are the reactants
- made by the reaction are the products.

During chemical reactions...
- new materials are made, but the total mass of the reactants is equal to the mass of the products
- no atoms are made or destroyed, they're just rearranged, so you say the mass is 'conserved'.

In the example below, by counting the different types of atom on each side of the equation, you can see that the mass of the reactants equals the mass of the products.

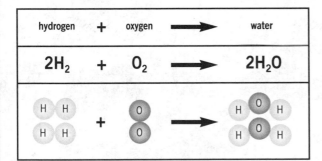

You'll see further examples of conservation of mass throughout this topic.

Burning Fuels

A **fuel** can be burned to release heat energy. Many fuels contain only carbon and hydrogen. These fuels are called **hydrocarbons**.

Three Examples of Fuels

Paraffin oil   Candle wax   Wood

Complete Combustion

Combustion is an example of an oxidation reaction. **Complete combustion** occurs when a hydrocarbon fuel is burned in a good supply of oxygen. When this happens...
- the carbon reacts with oxygen to form carbon dioxide
- the hydrogen reacts with oxygen to form water vapour.

This is the equation for the complete combustion of methane, the hydrocarbon fuel used by Bunsen burners:

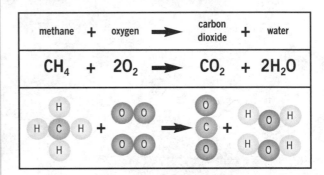

Candle wax is also a hydrocarbon fuel. The apparatus below can be used to test the gases produced when a candle is burned:
- The water vapour condenses to form a colourless liquid.
- The carbon dioxide turns the **limewater** cloudy.

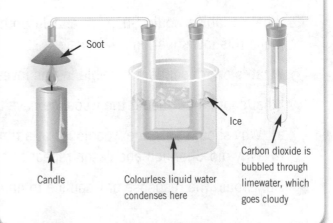

Soot

Ice

Candle

Colourless liquid water condenses here

Carbon dioxide is bubbled through limewater, which goes cloudy

Incomplete Combustion

Incomplete combustion occurs when a fuel is burned in a limited supply of oxygen. When this happens...
- there isn't enough oxygen available for the fuel to burn completely
- less heat energy is released
- the flame is yellow because it contains unburned carbon, which can be deposited on surfaces as soot
- a poisonous gas called carbon monoxide is produced. Carbon monoxide combines with the haemoglobin in red blood cells and stops them from being able to carry oxygen.

This is the equation for the incomplete combustion of methane:

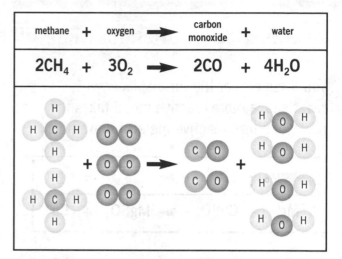

methane	+	oxygen	→	carbon monoxide	+	water
$2CH_4$	+	$3O_2$	→	$2CO$	+	$4H_2O$

Using Hydrogen as a Fuel

When hydrogen is burned...
- it reacts with oxygen to form water vapour
- lots of heat energy is released.

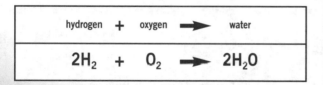

hydrogen	+	oxygen	→	water
$2H_2$	+	O_2	→	$2H_2O$

When hydrogen is burned, only water vapour is made. As the fuel doesn't contain carbon, carbon dioxide isn't produced. So, burning hydrogen doesn't add to the greenhouse effect.

Hydrogen is used as a fuel in rockets. As there's no air in space, rockets have to carry supplies of liquid hydrogen and liquid oxygen.

Matches

Matches can be used to light fires:
- A match head contains the elements carbon and sulfur, and the compound potassium chlorate ($KClO_3$). Compounds with names that end in 'ate' contain oxygen.
- Carbon and sulfur are fuels, and potassium chlorate is an oxidising agent. As the match head burns, the potassium chlorate releases oxygen that allows the two fuels to burn even better.

Self-Heating Cans

Climbers and explorers can now enjoy warm drinks straight from a can. These cans contain two sections:
- The top section contains the drink, for example coffee.
- The bottom section contains two chemicals that are kept separate by a thin layer of foil.
- When the thin foil is broken, the two chemicals react together. Heat energy is released and the coffee is warmed up.

Using Chemistry

Other Useful Chemical Reactions

You'll remember that in **displacement reactions**, a more reactive metal takes the place of a less reactive metal, for example:

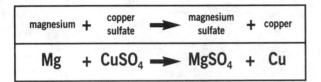

| magnesium | + | copper sulfate | → | magnesium sulfate | + | copper |

$$Mg + CuSO_4 \rightarrow MgSO_4 + Cu$$

Magnesium ribbon

Copper sulfate solution

Copper coating

Magnesium sulfate

Some of the chemical energy in the reactants is transferred into heat energy. As a result, the temperature of the solution increases.

In fact, the greater the difference in reactivity between the two metals in a displacement reaction, the more heat energy is released.

This energy can also be released as electrical energy. The voltage of a cell gives an indication of the energy released.

You can measure the voltage using a voltmeter:

- The greater the difference in reactivity between the two metals, the more energy is released, so the higher the voltage measured.
- If two pieces of the same metal are used, there's no difference in reactivity and no voltage is produced.

New Materials Made by Chemical Reactions

A huge range of materials are made by chemical reactions. Many of these materials are natural. For example, plants produce glucose by **photosynthesis**:

| carbon dioxide | + | water | → | glucose | + | oxygen |

However, some materials are made in factories. These are known as **synthetic materials** and many have very special uses.

New materials can benefit people enormously, but they must be carefully tested. For example, when a new medicine is developed, many years of tests are required in order to...
- check it's effective
- make sure it's safe to use and doesn't have dangerous side-effects
- work out the correct dose to treat patients.

Examples of Synthetic Materials

Shampoos – to remove dirt

Plastics – to make hundreds of things

Paint – to decorate and protect

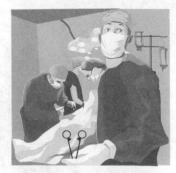

Anaesthetics – for painless operations

Zinc Reacting with Acid

Zinc metal reacts with dilute hydrochloric acid:

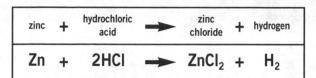

zinc	+	hydrochloric acid	→	zinc chloride	+	hydrogen
Zn	**+**	**2HCl**	**→**	**ZnCl₂**	**+**	**H₂**

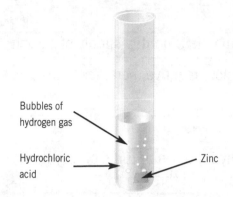

Bubbles of hydrogen gas

Hydrochloric acid

Zinc

The bubbles show that a gas is being made. As this gas escapes into the air, the mass of the test tube goes down. But the total mass of the products is the same as the total mass of the reactants, even when a gas is made.

Burning Magnesium

When magnesium is burned in air, the metal combines with oxygen to form the compound magnesium oxide:

magnesium	+	oxygen	→	magnesium oxide
2Mg	**+**	**O₂**	**→**	**2MgO**

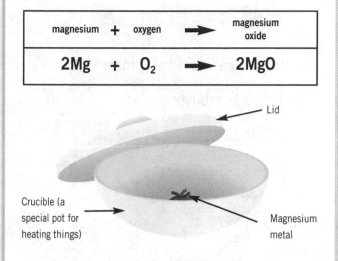

Lid

Crucible (a special pot for heating things)

Magnesium metal

The mass of the magnesium goes up because the magnesium has combined with oxygen, which has mass. However, the total mass of the reactants is still equal to the total mass of the products.

Burning Bread

Bread contains carbon and hydrogen. When bread is burned, the mass appears to go down as the carbon reacts with oxygen to form carbon dioxide gas and the hydrogen reacts with oxygen to form water vapour.

As the gases escape, the mass of the bread goes down but the overall mass is still conserved.

Quick Test

1. Define the term 'fuel'.
2. What are the products of the complete combustion of a hydrocarbon fuel?
3. Name the product of the combustion of hydrogen.
4. Where are synthetic materials made?
5. Explain what 'conservation of mass' means.
6. Why does the mass of magnesium go up when it's burned?

KEY WORDS
Make sure you understand these words before moving on!
- Complete combustion
- Displacement reaction
- Fuel
- Hydrocarbon
- Incomplete combustion
- Limewater
- Photosynthesis
- Synthetic material

Using Chemistry

Key Words Exercise

Match each key word to its meaning.

Complete combustion   •   •   When a material is burned in a limited supply of oxygen

Displacement reaction   •   •   A reaction in which a more reactive metal takes the place of a less reactive metal

Fuel   •   •   A material that's made in a factory

Hydrocarbon   •   •   A solution of calcium hydroxide that turns cloudy if carbon dioxide gas is bubbled through it

Incomplete combustion   •   •   The process by which green plants make glucose

Limewater   •   •   A substance that can be burned to release heat energy

Photosynthesis   •   •   When a material is completely burned in a good supply of oxygen

Synthetic material   •   •   A compound that contains only carbon and hydrogen

Comprehension

Read the passage about Joseph Priestley, then answer the following questions.

1. When was Joseph Priestley born?

2. Why was Joseph adopted?

3. Why is oxygen an important gas?

4. How is carbon dioxide used?

5. Why did Joseph have to leave his home?

6. What did Joseph do in America?

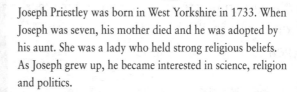

Joseph Priestley was born in West Yorkshire in 1733. When Joseph was seven, his mother died and he was adopted by his aunt. She was a lady who held strong religious beliefs. As Joseph grew up, he became interested in science, religion and politics.

He discovered the gas oxygen, which is needed for things to burn and for iron to rust. He also studied a gas produced at breweries by fermentation, which is now called carbon dioxide. Joseph found a way of dissolving the carbon dioxide into water. His discovery of carbonated water is widely used today in the manufacture of fizzy drinks. Joseph also discovered ammonia, sulfur dioxide and dinitrogen oxide or 'laughing gas'.

But when Joseph expressed support for the revolution that was happening in France, an angry mob attacked his home in Birmingham. Both his home and laboratory were destroyed. Joseph and his family fled to London, then to America. In America, Joseph established a church and continued his scientific work to improve people's lives.

Testing Understanding

1 **Fill in the missing words to complete the sentences about using chemistry.**

a) A _____ is a substance that can be burned to release heat energy. Many fuels contain only hydrogen and carbon and they're called _____ .

b) If a hydrocarbon fuel is burned in a limited supply of oxygen, _____ combustion occurs and carbon dioxide, carbon _____ and soot are produced.

c) When magnesium is added to copper sulfate, a displacement reaction takes place and _____ and _____ _____ are produced. During the reaction, _____ energy is released and the _____ of the solution increases. The greater the difference in reactivity between the two metals, the more _____ is released by the reaction.

d) During chemical reactions, new materials are _____ but the total mass of the _____ is equal to the total mass of the _____ . Atoms aren't created or destroyed, they are simply _____ .

2 **Read the information, then answer the questions that follow.**

Marianne carried out an investigation to find out how the mass of magnesium changes when it's burned. Her results are in the table below.

Experiment	Mass of Magnesium (g)	Mass of Magnesium Oxide (g)
1	0.50	0.82
2	0.30	0.50
3	0.10	0.16
4	0.26	0.32
5	0.16	0.26
6	0.42	0.69

a) Draw a graph to show Marianne's results. Remember to label each axis and include a line of best fit.

b) Describe the relationship between the mass of magnesium burned and the mass of magnesium oxide made.

c) One set of results doesn't fit the pattern. Circle this result on the graph and suggest why this result might be lower than expected.

Using Chemistry

Sarah is investigating how she can make an electrical cell from half a lemon and two pieces of metal. She connects the strips of metal to a voltmeter, which is used to indicate the energy produced by the electrical cell.

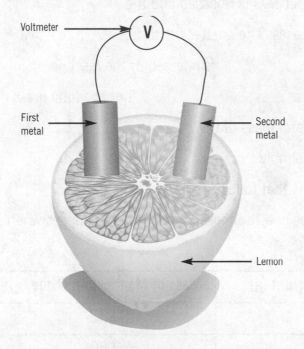

Voltmeter

V

First metal

Second metal

Lemon

Sarah used strips of magnesium, copper and iron in her experiment. Two different metals were used each time.

① Give the symbol used for each of these metals.
   a) The symbol for magnesium is _____
   b) The symbol for copper is _____
   c) The symbol for iron is _____

Sarah's results are shown in the table below.

② Copy and complete the table by adding headings for each column.

Iron and copper	0.78
Magnesium and copper	2.71
Iron and magnesium	1.93

③ Copy and complete the table below to show the variables that Sarah changed, measured and kept the same in her experiment.

Variable Changed	
Variable Measured	
Variable Kept the Same	

④ Draw a bar graph to display the results from Sarah's experiment.

The diagram below shows a section of the reactivity series.

Most reactive

Magnesium
Zinc
Iron
Copper

Least reactive

⑤ **a)** Which combination of different metals would produce the highest voltage?
   b) Which combination of different metals would produce the lowest voltage?
   c) Use the section of the reactivity series to suggest why these particular combinations of metals would produce the highest and lowest voltages.

Space and Gravity

Observing the Sky

Early observations of the sky helped people to understand time:

- Ancient civilisations studied the movement of the Sun, Moon and stars across the sky. These observations were used to measure time and the seasons, helping them to plan the planting and harvesting of crops.
- The Egyptians recognised fixed patterns of stars that appeared to move across the sky. By about 4000BC, they had developed the 365-day calendar.
- By about 1000BC, the Babylonians could predict the behaviour of the Moon and the planets in relation to distant constellations. Stonehenge was built in England, which lines up with the Sun's positions throughout the year.

The Geocentric Model

In 400BC, Aristotle realised that the Earth was a sphere and that different stars could be seen from different positions on the Earth's surface:

- Soon, the Pole Star, which is visible from all countries in the Northern Hemisphere, was being used to guide ships at sea.
- Aristotle wrongly believed that the Earth was the centre of the Universe and that the Sun, Moon, planets and stars moved around the Earth in circular orbits, supported by crystal spheres. This is known as a **geocentric** model.
- In 120AD, an Egyptian astronomer named Ptolemy developed a model of the Solar System, explaining Aristotle's ideas and agreeing that the Earth was at the centre.

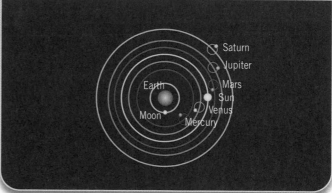

The Heliocentric Model

It wasn't until 1543 that Copernicus, from Poland, described a model for the Solar System with the Sun at the centre – a **heliocentric** model.

Church leaders of the time wouldn't accept the heliocentric model because they believed that God had put the Earth at the centre of the Universe.

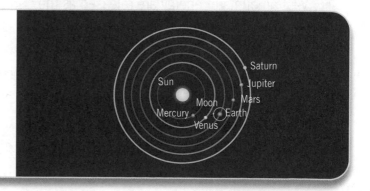

Space and Gravity

Improving the Model

When telescopes became more available, ideas began to change:

- In 1609, Kepler made observations and adapted Copernicus's model, changing the circular orbits of the planets around the Sun to elliptical orbits. Ellipses are squashed circles. This led to a greater understanding of how the speed of the planets changes as they orbit.
- There have been many other famous astronomers since, including Galileo and Hubble. The Hubble telescope has helped us to understand more about the movement of stars and galaxies in our Universe.

- Astronomers are still improving and adapting the model today as more information about our Universe is gathered.

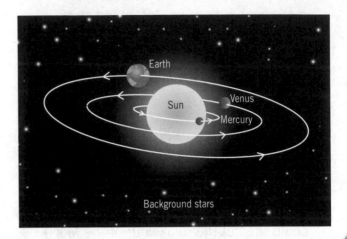

The Big Bang

Scientists today believe that the Universe began with a huge explosion called the **Big Bang**:

- In this explosion, energy, matter and forces came into being. Seconds later, everything began to cool and spread out.

- At this time, the force of gravity pulled together atoms of **hydrogen** and **helium** into clouds of gas and dust called **nebula**.
- Gravity pulled more gases together into stars, and pulled groups of stars into galaxies.

Inside a Star

Inside a star, the force of gravity pulls the gases together until the temperature and pressure are so great in the core that nuclear reactions occur:

- Vast amounts of energy are released as the star changes hydrogen into helium. Scientists have predicted that the Sun (a star) has enough hydrogen to keep it burning for 6000 million years!
- When a star's core has used up all of the available hydrogen fuel, the star's outer layer cools to a huge red ball called a **red giant**.

- Eventually the outer layer drifts away leaving a hot, dense core called a **white dwarf**. Later, the white dwarf also fades away as the star dies.
- Some stars are huge and instead of becoming a red giant, they explode. This explosion is known as a **super nova** and leaves behind a very small, dense **neutron star**.
- If an even larger star explodes, the gravity can be so strong that a **black hole** is formed. The gravity of a black hole is so strong that not even light can escape!

Gravity on Earth

Gravity is a force that acts between all objects that have mass. The force of gravity between two objects depends on...

- the mass of the objects (the greater their masses, the greater the force of gravity between them)
- the distance between the objects.

The force of gravity between two apples is too small to notice because apples have a small mass. The force of gravity between two planets is large because the planets are huge.

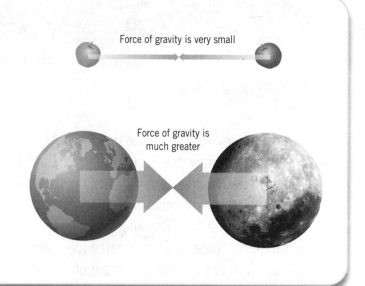

Force of gravity is very small

Force of gravity is much greater

Gravitational Force and Weight

The gravitational force between an object and the Earth is known as the weight of the object:

- On Earth, the force of gravity on an object (its weight) pulls it down.
- The weight of an object can be calculated using the gravitational field strength, which on Earth is equal to 10N/kg.

If something falls, it will fall with an acceleration caused by the force of gravity. This is called the acceleration of free fall.

It's said that Isaac Newton (1642–1727) saw an apple fall from a tree and accelerate under the force of gravity. He connected this force with the force that pulls the Moon towards Earth, keeping it in its orbit:

- Newton imagined the Moon to be continuously falling towards Earth, but never reaching it.
- He reasoned that the force of gravity kept the Moon falling and calculated how fast it would have to fall in order to keep orbiting the Earth, but to never reach it. When Newton made actual measurements of the motion of the Moon, he found that they matched his predictions.
- Newton showed that the force of gravity is what keeps objects in the Solar System in their orbits.

The Moon is pulled towards the Earth because it feels the gravitational field strength of the Earth. The Moon's gravity is felt weakly on Earth, but it's strong enough to affect the seas and oceans.

Tides are caused by the gravitational pull of the Moon. The gravitational pull of the Sun also affects the tides.

Space and Gravity

Satellites in Orbit

A force is required to change the direction of a moving object, such as the Earth rotating around the Sun. These forces are gravitational forces, and they hold planets and moons in their orbits:

- Planets close to the Sun experience large gravitational forces and their paths are curved.
- Planets further from the Sun experience weaker gravitational forces and follow less curved paths.

In the same way, an athlete has to exert a large inward force on a hammer to keep it going around in a circle. When he lets go, the force is no longer applied and the hammer moves away along a straight line.

Artificial satellites keep moving around the Earth without power:

- The only thing holding up satellites is the force of gravity from the Earth.
- A launch rocket takes the satellites into space and sets them into motion at the correct height and speed. A high orbit has a less curved path than a low orbit, so its speed can be less.

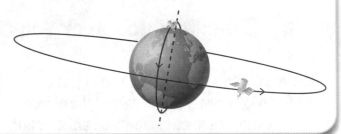

A Comet's Orbit

A comet has a highly-elliptical orbit around the Sun:

- When the comet is closest to the Sun, the gravitational force of the Sun on it is greatest and the comet speeds up.
- When the comet is furthest from the Sun, the gravitational force on it is weakest and the comet travels more slowly.

Quick Test

1. Who was the first person to suggest a heliocentric model?
2. Who opposed the heliocentric model and why did they oppose it?
3. What two things does the force of gravity between two objects depend on?
4. Why is the force of gravity between two apples very small?

KEY WORDS

Make sure you understand these words before moving on!

- Big Bang
- Black hole
- Geocentric
- Heliocentric
- Helium
- Hydrogen
- Nebula
- Neutron star
- Red giant
- Super nova
- White dwarf

Key Words Exercise

Match each key word with its meaning.

Key word	Meaning
Big Bang	A model of the Solar System with the Sun at the centre
Black hole	A model of the Solar System with the Earth at the centre
Geocentric	The gravity of this is so strong that not even light can escape
Heliocentric	The fuel of a star
Helium	A massive star dies in a big explosion known as this
Hydrogen	Scientists' model for the beginning of the Universe
Nebula	A star that has run out of fuel becomes this
Neutron star	The small, dense core of a dying star
Red giant	The dense core of a star left after a super nova
Super nova	A cloud of gas and dust
White dwarf	The product of a nuclear reaction inside a burning star

Comprehension

Read the passage about the astronomer, Edwin Hubble, then answer the following questions.

1. How did Edwin Hubble prove the existence of galaxies outside the Milky Way?

2. How did Hubble's observations change the accepted view of the Universe?

3. What other model did Hubble's work help scientists to develop?

4. What is special about the way that the Hubble telescope can be repaired?

The Hubble space telescope was carried into orbit by the space shuttle, Discovery, in 1990. It's named after the American astronomer, Edwin Hubble. Hubble discovered nebula in other galaxies outside the Milky Way, proving the existence of other galaxies and a Universe that was much larger than people believed. Many astronomers at the time opposed this idea. Hubble's observations changed the accepted view of the Universe.

Hubble also made measurements of the expanding Universe. His discoveries have helped scientists to develop the theory of the Big Bang. The Hubble telescope can be serviced by astronauts whilst in its orbit in space. It has been serviced four times and is still working today.

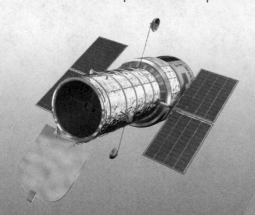

Space and Gravity

1 **Fill in the missing words to complete the sentences about space and gravity.**

   a) Inside a star, the force of _____ pulls gases together until the

   _____ and pressure are so great in the core that _____

   reactions occur. Vast amounts of _____ are released as the star changes

   hydrogen into _____ .

   b) When a star's _____ has used up all of the available

   _____ fuel, the star's outer layer cools to a _____ giant

   and leaves a hot, dense core called a _____ dwarf. Eventually, the white

   dwarf will also fade away as the star dies.

   c) Some stars are massive and instead of becoming a red giant, they _____ .

   This is known as a super nova. If an even larger star explodes, the _____

   can be so strong that a black hole is formed and not even _____ can escape!

2 **The diagram below shows the path of a comet travelling around the Sun.**

   a) What can you say about the gravitational pull of the Sun on the comet at A?
   b) What can you say about the gravitational pull of the Sun on the comet at B?
   c) What can you say about the speed of the comet at A?
   d) What can you say about the speed of the comet at B?

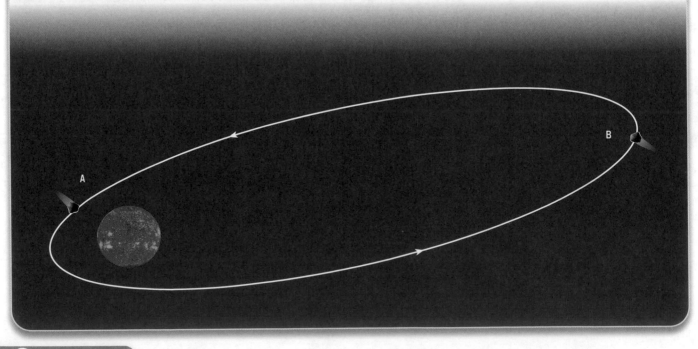

Abby wants to investigate the relationship between the force required to keep a satellite in orbit and its mass.

She plans to do this by setting up a model of a satellite orbiting the Earth. She will use different amounts of Plasticine attached to a string and spin them around. She will use a force sensor to measure the force required.

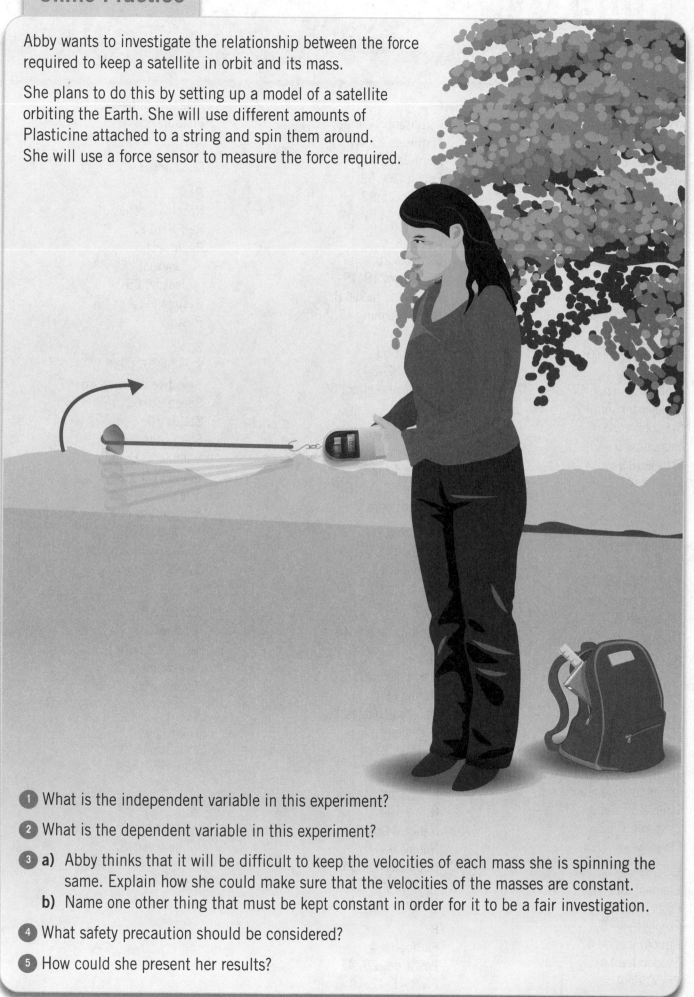

1. What is the independent variable in this experiment?

2. What is the dependent variable in this experiment?

3. a) Abby thinks that it will be difficult to keep the velocities of each mass she is spinning the same. Explain how she could make sure that the velocities of the masses are constant.

   b) Name one other thing that must be kept constant in order for it to be a fair investigation.

4. What safety precaution should be considered?

5. How could she present her results?

Index